Skyhorse Publishing books may be purchased in bulk at special discounts for sales promotion, corporate gifts, fund-raising, or educational purposes. Special editions can also be created to specifications. For details, contact the Special Sales Department, Skyhorse Publishing, 307 West 36th Street, 11th Floor, New York, NY 10018 or info@skyhorsepublishing.com.

Skyhorse® and Skyhorse Publishing® are registered trademarks of Skyhorse Publishing, Inc.®, a Delaware corporation.

Visit our website at www.skyhorsepublishing.com.

10 9 8 7 6 5 4 3 2 1

Library of Congress Cataloging-in-Publication Data is available on file.

Food Styling by Elena Richards

Cover design by Qualcom Designs
Cover photo credits: Judah Gutierrez, Arrie B. Bowden, iStock, and Associated Press

ISBN: 978-1-51074-352-6
Ebook ISBN: 978-1-51074-354-0

Printed in China

To Jess, for the idea, and for Fletch, who never stops believing.

In the ideas, or, in me.

CONTENTS

Part I: The Outward 9

I shall be telling this with a sigh
Somewhere ages and ages hence:
Two roads diverged in a wood, and I—
I took the one less traveled by,
And that has made all the difference.
—Robert Frost
Circa 1915

AUGUSTA & ME: THE MAKINGS OF AN UNLIKELY FRIENDSHIP

My love affair with Augusta National began more than four decades ago, at the tender age of 10. During those formidable years, I came to know her in ways unlike anyone before me. Or since.

We grew up together, Augusta and me. No, not during the days of Bobby Jones standing on muddy tee boxes, ripping drives into the wild blue yonder to determine where to place bunkers, plant pines, or move mounds of red Georgia clay, but in the '70s, when Evel Knievel was breaking bones as fast as Jack was breaking par. A time when parking lots were gravel, and the waiting list for Masters badges was something you got on, not something you waited to get on.

We were green as the wax paper cups that overflowed with Coca-Cola, Augusta and me. As green as the refrigerated bent grass that replaced Bermuda on the fastest surface this side of melting ice cream. We were ticket windows with tickets for sale, gallery guards holding yellow ropes as suggestions, not commands.

We were the back-9-only televised, sixty-second commercials that held your attention, practice round tickets laying on Formica kitchen counters, a single black-and-white TV on a worn, wooden desk in the caddy masters' office—an office that doubled as storage for the pro shop, with members' clubs stacked in corners like so many organized matchsticks. We were local caddies who knew the course like bloodhounds know the trail, cold or hot. We were the beginning of the end of a golden age, Augusta and me.

And, man, did it feel good to be both.

—Tripp Bowden, 17 July 2018

INTRODUCTION

They say there's an art to great cooking. I won't argue that point. There's an art to everything, from bubble gum blowing to kickball to preaching to the choir to orthopedic surgery. But you don't have to be Rembrandt or Picasso to be a great artist (ever heard of Bob Ross?), just like you don't have to be Julia Child or Paul Prudhomme to be a great cook. You've just got to be you.

It's easier than you've been led to believe.

I have no professional training with Pampered Chef garlic presses or Le Creuset Dutch ovens; no Cooking 101 certificates of achievement hang from the walls of my man cave. But that hasn't stopped me from cooking like Justin Wilson with a Category 4 of frenzy fast approaching, filling my family's kitchen with the succulent smells of fried pork chop sandwiches and collard greens, or peppercorn crusted filets with glistening Parisian potatoes and grill-marked Italian bread.

And it shouldn't stop you.

If it has, consider this cookbook the ultimate set of culinary jumper cables—a road map to the land of great eats. Go where you want to go; tackle the interstate or boot scoot down the backroads; take on the road less traveled or the road not traveled at all. I'm cool with either. Just promise me you'll take one—or as Sean Penn's Spicoli character once said to the brother of a young Forest Whitaker in the '80s-defining teen comedy *Fast Times at Ridgemont High*, "You drive, I'll navigate."

Given the fact that both Penn and Whitaker went on to win Best Actor at the Academy Awards, surely there must be a sliver of truth in such sage advice.

When it comes to cooking, I'm not into exact measurements, not a huge fan of saying, well, this dish calls for a ¼ teaspoon of that, a ⅓ tablespoon of this, an ounce of I'm not gonna eat it, and a pound of you just cured my appetite for life. But I'm King Kong big into making sure *this,* and *that,* are in *there.* If you grew up in a home where meals were made with a pinch, a dab, a drizzle, and a splash, this is the cookbook for you.

Oh, can you promise me one more thing? Pretty please, with a cherry (or whatever you wish) on top?

Once you've tried these recipes the way they're rolled out on these pages, promise me the next time you make them, you make them your own. This is just a road map, remember? Take whatever exit you like.

You'll get there.

JUST ANSWER THE QUESTION, YOUNG MAN

(BUT WHERE'S THE FUN IN THAT?)

Why?

Why do we all own at least *one* cookbook, even though we may not know a cream-filled doughnut from crème brûlée?

What is it about eating a dirty water dog on the corner of 81st and 3rd with a New York summer shower splashing our skin, or dining with friends over a shared appy of Oysters Rockefeller at 21 Club that somehow, defying all logic and reason, puts a smile on our face we simply cannot take off?

What is it about food that brings us together, regardless of race, color, background, or creed? Why does the vast majority of things we do, say, share, and celebrate so often involve food—and lots of it?

Because good food makes us happy, that's why!

From street corners to street lamps, from Zagat zealots to holes in the wall, good food makes us happy. It's no different the world over, even within the hallowed walls of Augusta National's iconic dining room, land of imported Italian olives the size of strawberries and an endless sea of Lafite Rothschild, name the year, forget the price. Or at Augusta's picnic-tabled, cinder block caddy house, where fried pork chop sandwiches and southern style butterbeans once ruled the roost—good food is good food.

It doesn't matter where you find it, so long as you do.

If you are what you eat, then I only want to eat the good stuff!
—Remy, from the movie Ratatouille

PART I
THE OUTWARD 9

bypass: / bi pas /
NOUN
a road passing around a town or its center to provide an alternative route
for through traffic
VERB
to go past or around
—*Oxford Living English Dictionary*

By now, it should be hand-smacked-by-the-nun's-ruler obvious this isn't your typical cookbook. But that's a good thing; in fact, that's a great thing. If you've gotten this far turning glossy pages, processing unexpected words, and kicking your brain into a gear you forgot you had, chances are *you* ain't the typical cook.

That, too, is a very good thing.

Speaking of, the only thing we're gonna bypass on this edible adventure is boredom. So, strap on your seatbelt, don't forget where you came from, and let the fur fly!

BY THE POWER VESTED IN ME

Few people know Augusta National the way I do. As a young lad, I spent many a summer (until golf seduced my wandering soul) fishing her waters for bream and bass, catching Bible-sized bream by the dozens, the bass only when they felt like biting, as they had the same sort of patience as me: very little. But when you're in the process of coming of age (does that process ever truly end?), standing still is nothing short of impossible.

"Fishing the waters of Augusta" might ring a little heavy on *The Old Man and the Sea*, but it also rings quite true, at least in my little boy memory. My fishing pole may have been cane and not deep sea, and the only thing strapping me in was the seat of my shorts touching the ryegrass banks of the Par Three Course, but some of the best fishing in the world, if not *the* best (and by that I also mean the most fun), can be found at Augusta National.

In those halcyon days, Augusta's ponds were teeming with fish, and I would pull them in hand over fist as the very lucky guest of Freddie Bennett, Caddy Master of Augusta National Golf Club for over 40 years. From my vantage point, Freddie knew more about Augusta than Clifford Roberts and Bobby Jones—the two men who founded the place!

I've written at length about my experiences at Augusta, both in my first book *Freddie & Me: Life Lessons from Freddie Bennett, Augusta National's Legendary Caddy Master* and *All the Memorable Rounds: Golf Adventures and Misadventures from Augusta National to Cypress Point and Beyond*. Of *Freddie & Me*, the *New York Times* reckoned: "A lot of books have been written about the Masters and Augusta National Golf Club, but few if any have the authentic dialect of *Freddie & Me*." Golf icon and legendary PGA Tour television commentator and analyst Ben Wright, a man of well-chosen words, had this to say about *All the Memorable Rounds*: "What a fine collection of tales."

Kind words, indeed. But that's not why I write.

In *Freddie & Me*, I touched on the tasty eats found in both the caddy house and clubhouse of Augusta, but those were just the skeletons of what I know. The book you're holding puts meat on the ol' girl's bones and takes her out dancing. Sometimes it's ballroom, sometimes sawdust floor, but I can promise you this: in *The Caddy's Cookbook*, that girl is getting her groove on.

Shall we dance?

CADDY HOUSE CUISINE

Horace Avery may have come from humble beginnings (think no running water and a woodburning stove), but the food he could whip up behind the metal screen that separated Augusta's caddy house cook from those in need of some serious cooking was anything but. That's not to say Horace's menu was highly involved or overly complex—in fact, it was just the opposite, as simple as a shoelace. But when it came to pleasing the palate of rode hard and put up wet caddies who likely hadn't eaten so much as a pack of Nip Chee crackers since they walked out that hanging-hinge caddy yard gate, Horace's eats were eats for the ages.

My first steps into the caddy world of Augusta National Golf Club were and still are baby ones, having first set foot inside that chain-linked caddy yard green as the grass that abuts it. It's a Masters Monday, my very first one.

With the sun creeping up in the sky and my dad leading the way, I follow his footsteps like dew drops down tree bark as Pop zigs and zags through a throng of people in pursuit of that sea of green grass, before taking a sharp right turn through an open iron gate guarded by speed bumps of red Georgia clay.

As we make our way through a collage of white jumpsuits, brown skin, and green hats, a chorus of, "Hey Doc," "All right now, Doc," "What's shakin' Doc?" and "My man, Doc!" surrounds us like a hive of friendly bees with honey from the rock. I can't help but bow up like a bantam. That's *my* dad they're talking about!

I wonder why?

More quickly followed footsteps take me through the front door (there is no back or side door that I can tell) of the caddy house and inside unknown territory. Pop walks up to a faded blue—so faded it looks gray—laminate countertop and taps on a metal grid window. It looks like the pay window at a horse race, and with my stomach rumbling like a blown speaker, I can't help but wonder if we're about to win, place, or show.

"Hey, Horace. You alive in there?"

Nothing. Just the sound of caddy-speak behind us:

"Son, the only tip your man gonna give you is telling your no caddying ass to go smash somebody else's grass!"

"Shit, I ain't been fired since Grover Cleveland was President."

"The only Grover you know is that trash can fool on *Sesame Street*. Now gimme my five dollars so I can get me a pork chop sandwich and some butterbeans. My ass got some hills to walk today. But that ain't nothing you'd know about."

It's like another language, this caddy-speak, and it's the most beautiful sound I've ever heard. I turn around to face the steel window. Pop knocks again.

"Ah, damnit! What y'all crazy som'bitches be wanting now?" A face that must be Horace leans down and peers through the metal. "Aw, now. Hey, Doc. How you doin'? I ain't seen you—"

"Since the last time you saw me!"

"Hey, heh. Yeah, that be about right, Doc. You lookin' good now. Must be all that clean living."

"I wash up every time I operate, Horace. Oh, by the way, you're next."

"Oh, hell no," says Horace. "The only knife getting near me is the one I'm holding." Horace lifts a hefty knife that looks like it's been used for cutting bone, and I don't mean chicken. The big blade gleams in the fluorescent light. If I were any closer, I could see my reflection. I can certainly smell the fear.

"Say, is that your boy there, Doc?"

Pop nods and smiles, his thin red hair bouncing off his forehead. "Tripper, say hello to Horace Avery, caddy house cook extraordinaire. Horace, meet my son Tripp."

"Fruit of your loins, lemme tell you. He looks just like you, Doc."

"Of course, he does. He's good-looking, ain't he?"

Horace laughs and taps the knife handle on the counter, points the tip at Doc, and smiles. Sort of. If a stone could smile, this would be it.

"And let me tell you, Horace. This little man can eat!"

Horace sizes me up, all 4 feet, 86 pounds of me.

"Where the hell's he puttin' it? Hollow leg or something?"

"Oh, it's something all right." Pop reaches down with his big mitt, palms my right shoulder, and motions me to the counter so close I can touch it, but I don't. No, sir. I can feel Horace's eyes on me, still not sure what to make of what they see. Pop holds up two fingers. Two bubbling grape sodas appear as if by magic, and Horace disappears.

But Horace is far from finished with us.

"One deep fried pork sandwich for you, one deep fried pork chop sandwich for me."

Pop hands me a heavy square of loosely folded wax paper, green as the grass beneath our feet. I've sipped mightily on the grape soda he handed me back at the caddy house, and by the time we make it to the metal bleachers overlooking the east practice tee, I've got nothing left but a burning throat (it's a good burn) and ice. Pop stares down into my empty cup.

"To keep it from spilling," I say, looking up at my dad, as if that's the answer to the question he wants to ask.

"Well, where's the fun in that?" says Pop, smiling as we take front-row seats. We settle in, the metal bleachers warm from the rising sun that now feels like it's in my lap.

Pop unwraps his pork chop sandwich just enough to let the sunlight cast a ray on a glistening section of fried goodness. I do the same. Two big bites later and we're both

smiling to beat the band. A couple of men in knee-draping Bermuda shorts and black socks are fidgeting in the seats behind us, staring over our shoulders like two vultures wanting one from the road. If I had eyes in the back of my head (like my mom!) I would see sandwiches in their hands, too. Only their sandwiches are very different from the ones Pop and I are holding—one egg salad, one pimento cheese. Both men have stopped chewing.

Pop, however, has not.

"Ah, yes," he says, holding his pork chop sandwich high in the air for all the world to see, especially the two tourists behind us. "The breakfast of champions!"

With his sandwich still sky-high, Pop peels back more wax paper to reveal a bone-in pork chop big enough to feed the five thousand. I do the same, and again we dig in but with bigger bites this time, the warm juice dripping down our fingers and onto the ryegrass below. A few drops land on time-polished bleachers, and it's hard to tell which shines the brightest—the grass, the bleachers, or me.

One pair of black socks turns to the other and whispers in a voice he thinks I can't hear, "Where in the heck did they get *those*?"

I'll never tell.

HORACE AVERY'S LEGENDARY FRIED PORK CHOP SANDWICHES

[FEEDS 8]

INGREDIENTS AND TOOLS OF THE TRADE

- Family-sized pack of bone-in pork chops (center cut for Augusta members; bone-in pork loin thin cut for caddies and grounds crew. Personal preference? Hands down the bone-in pork loin, thin cut. They give a little extra on the juice, marbling, and overall flavor).
- Roasting pan for holding and seasoning the chops.
- Salt (Morton's table salt will suit just fine).
- Coarse ground pepper (16 mesh is best, but straight out of the old shaker works, too).
- Tongs for putting the chops in and taking them out of really hot oil, unless you want to burn that mother down (that would be your fingers).
- Flour (White Lily or Dixie.) If you have some handy, go with House-Autry, Southern-crafted goodness since 1812. Try the chicken or seafood breading—doesn't matter which one. Both work wonders.
- Old-school cast iron skillet, electric fryer, or FryDaddy.
- Oil (vegetable or peanut is fine. Anything but baby).
- Paper towels for the fried chops.
- Large plate or cookie sheet on which to place said paper towels.
- White bread (Colonial King Thin, Nature's Own Artisan, or Sunbeam).
- Hot sauce, Texas Pete, or Frank's RedHot Original.

PREPARATION

Rip open the family-sized package of chops. (It's fun to rip things open!) No need to rinse. Place the chops an inch or so apart in a roasting pan, or any tool of the trade that is about three inches deep. A Ziploc bag works, too, but can be messier than a three-year-old with a box of melted crayons.

Season the chops with salt and pepper. We've all heard the phrase: season to taste. Well, I say season until you get it right for *you*. Not for anyone else but you—unless you're cooking for little ones. In that case, forget the chops and go straight for the ice cream.

Once seasoned, flip the chops with tongs or your washed hands. Season again. Now, coat both sides of the chops with either flour or House-Autry breading mix. A light coating is best in my eyes—we ain't baking cakes here.

Add oil to your cast iron skillet (about a knuckle deep throughout), or deep or electric fryer (look for the tell-tale fill line and do not, I repeat, do not cross unless you're trying to earn a clean-up-one-hell-of-a-mess merit badge). Or, add the oil to your FryDaddy (in my case, a Fry *Grand Pappy* that has done more frying in the past 40 years than a redheaded sunbather).

Heat the oil to 350. Don't have a frying thermometer? That's ok—neither do I. Just take a pinch (there's that word again) of flour—or water drops (chemistry majors beware)—and flick 'em into the warming oil. If they bubble and pop or otherwise get your attention, you're good to go.

Once the oil is ready for frying, gently place the chops into the swirling goodness using tongs, one chop then another. Fry no more than two chops at a time, regardless of skillet or fryer space. Like an old married couple, fried pork chops need room to breathe, and since they cook up faster than a down-grain three-footer at Augusta, these juicy darlings will be ready in no time!

Let the chops fry for 2–3 minutes, then ease one out and check the firmness of the meat, how it bends off the bone. You want just a little give—that means she's done but still tender and juicy. But if they're not quite ready, ease 'em back into the oil for another minute, two at the most.

I wish there were shortcuts for knowing when a fried chop is a ready chop, but there aren't any this side of *knowing* already. And the only way to know already is to have *done it* already. Well, guess what? Now, you have.

Take those life lessons out of the fryer and lay 'em side by side on a paper-toweled plate or cookie sheet. Repeat. But if you don't know from which step, I ain't telling you.

Advice about Serving Suggestions: *I once saw an ad where the headline read: "Suggested retail price: $90," and it was an ad for a basic button-down shirt. Beneath that headline were the words: "We have a suggestion for whoever suggested that!" with a picture of that button-down shirt giving the "suggestion" the ol' F-U! Lesson to be learned here? Take all suggestions with a grain of salt—and sometimes the whole shaker.*

SERVING SUGGESTION (ACTUAL)

Place each fried pork chop on a slice of white bread—don't let anyone see you do this, but take the slices from the middle of the loaf—they're the softest and the freshest. Top the chops with whatever sauce or condiment you want: Texas Pete, Frank's, A1, Heinz 57, mustard, mayo, more salt and pepper, or a whole lot of nothing. Toppings don't hurt my feelings, but if you've done it right, then a whole lot of nothing might just be the only topping you'll need.

Put the standby slice on top of the chop and gently squish down (*press*, for you non-slangladites) the sandwich with bended knuckles. Voilà, my friend. You've done it!

The black socks are green with envy.

PERFECT POT LIQUOR

DEBUNKING THE MYTH THAT IT'S
A PAIN IN THE ASS TO MAKE

The insightful and dry-witted Robert Fulghum coined the phrase "All I really need to know, I learned in kindergarten." Whether or not the phrase is original to Fulghum doesn't matter. Like the gent who came up with the sticky note, ol' Robert took his idea to the masses and ran all the way to the bank.

A good idea is a good idea.

Robert also penned a lovely book by the same name that is filled with some of the most obvious life lessons imaginable—and the most ignored: "Clean up your own mess." "Play fair." "Put things back where you found them." "Live a balanced life—learn some and think some and draw and paint and sing . . . and work every day some."

Oh, I almost forgot. Share *everything*.

The same can be said for pot liquor. There is *no* good cuisine, Southern or otherwise, without it. Just like there is no football without the forward pass, no golf without the three-foot putt, no dictionary without Webster, and by God and for the love of all that's liquid, there is simply no cooking without pot liquor.

And what good is perfect pot liquor if you don't share the recipe?

The good news is that making perfect pot liquor is a hell of a lot easier than most cooks have been letting on and leading other folks to believe for the past 2,000-plus years (give or take a parted Red Sea and a trip down T-Rex Lane). Don't believe me?

Try this simple recipe and see how easy making perfect pot liquor really is.

11

PERFECT POT LIQUOR, CADDY YARD STYLE

(SERVES ONE DISH AT A TIME)

INGREDIENTS AND TOOLS OF THE TRADE

- 32-ounce plastic cup (one that can handle the microwave and dishwasher).
- Chicken bouillon, preferably Goya or bust.
- Pepper vinegar.
- McCormick garlic salt—California style with parsley.
- Red wine vinegar.
- Chicken stock, preferably Kitchen Basics or Kirkland organic.
- Ground pepper.
- McCormick lemon pepper.
- Gruet blanc de noirs methode champenoise, or your favorite chardonnay.
- Agave sweetener, spoonful of sugar, or a couple packs of Sweet-n-Low or Splenda.
- Juice of half a lemon (use a lemon squeezer, if you have one).

PREPARATION

In a proper, microwave-safe 32-ounce plastic cup—like the souvenir kind from beach trips or ballgames—add in a little Goya chicken bouillon and a dash or two of pepper vinegar. Throw in a couple shakes of garlic salt, a few douses of the red wine vinegar, a long pour or two of the chicken stock. Shake in some ground pepper and lemon pepper. Pour in a shot of champagne and a few drops of agave. Squeeze in the lemon juice. Stir. Your liquid level should be about halfway up the cup. If you want to add a splash of H2O, feel free.

Pop it in the microwave for five minutes. If you've got one of those flat plastic square covers or even a small dish, put it on top of your 32-ounce cup of pot liquor magic. Might save you from making a mess and getting an ass-chewing.

When the time's up, let the goodness sit in the microwave for a couple more ticks of the clock. That's where the true cooking comes from in a microwave, but they don't tell you that in the check-out line at Walmart.

I learned that from my mama.

My family had the first-ever microwave in our provincial Dorchester neighborhood in Augusta, Georgia, circa 1973. And what a microwave it was! Imagine a Samsonite suitcase, but with a large glass window, knobs, and plugs. Kids would come from far and wide to nuke hot dogs, boil soup, and blow up eggs in that old-school food heater.

Pop used to joke, "Son, you could cook an elephant in this thing!"

Now that you've given your cup o' goodness her two minutes in a neutral corner (in this case the sealed confines of your microwave), open the door and ease her out. Be careful; the cup might be hot (and the small plate too, if that's what you used to cover). In fact, there's a very good chance it'll be *damn* hot, so grip the cup as close to the rim as you can without spilling it. Now, grab your favorite spoon and give that juice a taste but blow on it before you do, or you'll be licking bandages for the next week.

Did you nail it? I'll bet you did.

FROM THE CADDY MASTER TO THE KID

It's the summer of my 10th year of life, and I'm sitting at the kitchen table of my parents' new house, spooning chili that's mild as a breeze into my mouth and staring out a bay window with yellow curtains and patchwork flowers. My mom is a great cook, Southern as a bowl of collards. Whatever she cooks, I eat.

Some folks were raised on radio. I was raised on fatback.

I'm also lost as a set of keys, having moved from a neighborhood where I knew everyone to a neighborhood where I know no one. I've gone from Pied Piper to pie-in-the-face, when along comes Freddie Bennett to clean up the mess that is me.

There's a knock on our back door, solid raps that seem thought out. The knuckles attached to the hand that's knocking must be grapefruit big. I peer around the corner, frozen in my tracks. Freddie's smile thaws me out, and I open the unlocked back door. I grew up with unlocked doors, on houses and cars. My Nan always said, "Grandson, locks are for honest people."

I open the door a little wider.

"Hey, man. It's Freddie. My doctor home?"

He says these words as if I must know who he is, as if I've known him all my life.

"Sure," I say, and open the door that leads to the garage all the way, flush to the frame so Freddie can get through, all broad shoulders and Popeye arms that he is.

He's a solid mammoth of a man, this Freddie, and mighty handsome, too, sporting creased black pants, Guccis with no socks, and a just-off-the-rack white golf shirt with a map of the United States above the left breast, a yellow flag sticking out of Georgia.

Beneath that logo are two words that will one day change my life: Caddy Master.

It takes a moment before I realize Freddie has offered his hand to me. I reach for it, clumsy and awkward. Freddie's big hand swallows mine, but his handshake is warm and welcoming. It is the first handshake I remember.

"Your dad," he says. "He's home?"

My dad. I almost forgot!

I turn to hear Pop's distinct voice, booming and baritone, as familiar as a toothbrush. It's all bass notes and enunciation, and you can hear it all the way to the mailbox.

"Heyyy, Freddie! What's shakin', my man?" Pop walks over and cups Freddie on the shoulder, like a Baptist preacher at a meet and greet.

"Everything's good, Doc." Freddie nods his head and smiles as he and Doc shake hands. "Just thought I'd swing by and see if maybe you could check my ticker, just in case I forgot to wind it. I've been one busy mother lately."

"Sure thing, man. How 'bout the plumbing?"

"Well, if I'm a quart low I don't want to know about it."

I sit back down at the table, laughing, though I'm not really sure at what.

"What'cha sitting down for, Smoke? Let's go—you're coming with us."

With you? *Where?* I'm never invited when adults are involved.

Pop motions for Freddie, and for the first time ever *me*, to join him in his office, which doubles as our den. We belly up to the bar, a wooden slab of mahogany with metal edges that rise to keep drinks from sliding over the edge. My drink is an 8-ounce bottled Coke (much better than in the can), and Pop eases off the cap with the deftness of the surgeon that he is.

Freddie signals with three thick fingers and smiles as Pop pours a generous flow of Cutty Sark into Freddie's highball and then his own. Freddie swirls the glass as Pop quickly gets to work pumping up the crinkly blood pressure brace, accentuating Freddie's massive bicep. Freddie acts as if it's not even there, but I can't take my eyes off the cuff as it bulges like a life raft.

"Changing the greens over to bent, Doc. I knew it was coming. Just a matter of time—never a matter of money. Not with those cats. To tell you the truth, I never understood going with Bermuda in the first place. That thick-ass grass is for croquet and walking barefoot. Augusta's greens were built for speed, man. Designed to make you three-putt your liver out before they take your no-playing-ass off the leaderboard and the plane ticket out of your pocket. Sodding those slopes with Bermuda was like putting cookie dough on an exit ramp."

Pop laughs like Howdy Doody with puberty in the rearview mirror, a pitch of lows and lowers. I'd laugh, too, if I knew what the heck Freddie was talking about.

Pop releases the pump and the cuff deflates like a dollar float in the kiddie pool.

Freddie slides it off his arm like he's shooing a fly.

"Shoot it to me straight, Doc. I'm dying, ain't I?"

"Yes, but not anytime soon. Your ticker is strong as a horse."

"Secretariat or Mr. Ed?" asks Freddie. This time I laugh, too. This joke I get.

"Well, the verdict is still out on the rest of you," says Pop, smiling. He raises the water level on Freddie's glass another finger, then two. Freddie swirls his highball in tight circles on the bar, turns his stool to face me, and pushes the glass aside. Pop is now angled out of my line of sight, though I'm not sure he knows it.

"Hey, man. I hear you don't like golf. But I hear you like to fish?"

Even though Freddie's looking right at me, it doesn't sink in that he's talking to me. A pause hangs in the air, like bats in a cave.

"Son, Freddie's talking to you."

"Sir?" I've been so entranced with Freddie's curious hold on the King's English it's like I've forgotten how to speak.

"He's asking you about fishing."

"Oh, yes, sir. Yes, I *love* to fish. I, I got a new Zebco for Christmas. It's a closed face—just press down with your thumb and cast, far as you want." My eyes drop to the shag carpet. Closed face. How stupid do *I* sound? Of course, my Zebco is closed face. They don't make an open one.

Freddie smiles. Maybe he didn't hear me.

"Well, that settles it then. Tomorrow we're going fishing. At the Club, if that's all right with you." Freddie turns, winks at Pop. "Y'know, that Zebco sounds nice, sounds like Santa likes you a lot and I'm betting what's not to like, but you don't need that fancy thing where we're going. It'll only slow you down. Where we're going, you'll catch 'em so fast you'll be thinking the pond's on fire!"

Only slow me down? A pond on fire? Say what?

"Oh, wow," is all I can manage.

"I'd say wow, too, son, if I was going fishing at the Club."

"Best fishing in the world," says Freddie, turning to face me. "You ain't never seen anything like it, man. Ain't that right, Doc?"

"Right as rain," says Pop, but all I can think of is when's the last time Pop went fishing? It sure as heck wasn't with me.

"How's nine o'clock sound?" says Freddie. "I'll pick you up first thing." He turns and takes the smallest sip of scotch. "That all right with you, Doc?"

"Absolutely. Tripper here's got nothing planned, unless you call sleeping till noon and wasting your youth a plan." Pop laughs and musses my hair.

He's being funny, but he's also telling the truth.

Pop lifts his scotch off the bar, leans back in his chair, and lets out an envious sigh. "How about that," he says, an east-west grin across his face. "Fishing Ike's Pond with the man himself. Boy, I'd swap out all my scalpels for a day at the Club like that."

The expression on my face says I should know what the "Club" is, but I don't.

"That would be the *Augusta National Golf Club*," says Pop, beaming. The expression on his face says that should mean something to me, but it doesn't.

My life was about to change forever, but I didn't know that either.

Freddie was right.

Few people know this, and even fewer would believe me, but some of the best— if not *the* best fishing in the world—is at Augusta National Golf Club. Especially during the dog days of summer, when the bream are on bed, the course closed to everyone except you and the caddy master (you'll soon come to learn nothing at Augusta is closed, off-limits, or kept secret from *this* caddy master), and the ponds wide open.

You'll also soon learn that Freddie is as much the caretaker of Augusta National as he is the caddy master. There's nothing he doesn't know about this place; it's like the Nicene Creed: And from him no secrets are hid. That would be pretty hard to do, since Freddie is the one keeping them in the first place.

Freddie was right—did I say that already? Well, I've never seen anything like it before or since.

With my glistening red Zebco safe in the bedroom closet back home, I pull in bream after bream with a bamboo cane pole Freddie made himself from a live cane he cut down just the day before. There's an impenetrable forest of the hearty stuff to the right of number 4 at Augusta, the beastly par three with the only palm tree on the course (it's up on the bank, to the right of the green). But that's not what's impressive about number 4 at Augusta. The hundreds of water moccasins living in the thicket of sky-high bamboo guarding the right side of the fairway are what's impressive. As Freddie later tells me: "Don't ever go in there, man. I don't care if you're following Jesus Christ!"

To this day I still wonder how Freddie was able to go in there without getting bit eight ways to Sunday.

IKE'S POND DEEP-FRIED BREAM

INGREDIENTS AND TOOLS OF THE TRADE, PART I

(Author's note: If you're a bit squeamish when it comes to blood and guts, have someone do this part for you.)

- IKE'S POND. CHANCES ARE, THIS AIN'T HAPPENING, SO ANY POND WILL DO JUST FINE, LONG AS THERE'RE FISH IN IT.
- FISH. BREAM ARE WHAT WE PULLED OUT OF IKE'S POND, BUT ANY FISH WILL DO IF THERE'S GOOD MEAT ON THEIR BONES, SUCH AS CRAPPIE OR BASS.
- A MIGHTY SHARP KNIFE (ONE WE WILL RETURN TO THROUGHOUT THIS COOKBOOK).
- A SPOON, LIKE THE ONE YOU USE TO EAT CEREAL. IF YOU HAVE A SO-CALLED FISH SCALER, PLEASE GIVE IT AWAY IMMEDIATELY TO SOMEONE YOU DON'T PARTICULARLY LIKE ANYMORE, OR WON'T LIKE YOU, ONCE YOU GIVE IT TO THEM.
- NEWSPAPER. YESTERDAY'S OR TODAY'S.
- SOMETHING IN WHICH TO PUT THE FISH GUTS.
- HOSE WITH A GOOD NOZZLE ON IT.
- CARD OR PICNIC TABLE.
- A PLACE WHERE YOU CAN USE THAT HOSE TO SPRAY THE TABLE, CLEANING OFF FISH BITS AND SCALES, AND KEEPING THE WIFE HAPPY.

PREPARATION

Pull a shiny bream from the cooler (be sure they aren't sticky) and lay it on the table. Get a good grip and slice off the head with your very sharp knife. If you're deft with the blade, hold the fish where the fins are facing north and you're standing south, or east and you west, with one hand on the head and the other on the handle of your very sharp knife.

Remove the head. Slice open the belly about an inch along the bottom of the fish. The entrails should come out relatively easy, though you may have to tug a little, like you would a lamp cord from the socket, and you at a weird angle on the couch.

Repeat the above until all the fish are headed and gutted. Take your spoon with the rounded edge and scrape from east to west against the scales—from tail to head, or at least where the head used to be. Be sure to scrape the top and bottom of your fish. When you're finished, that fish should be smooth as the skin on the moccasins taking up residence on the 4th hole at Augusta.

Rinse your fish. Not once but twice.

If you want me to say gently pat the fish dry with a paper towel or soft cloth, sorry. I'm not going to. These ain't mushrooms; these are fish.

Step back now and admire your handiwork. Few things are more beautiful than a mess of cleaned fish ready for the fryer.

INGREDIENTS AND TOOLS OF THE TRADE, PART II

- LARGE PAN OR POT FOR BREADING THE FISH.
- FISH BREADING, LIKE HOUSE-AUTRY, OR, IF YOU WANT TO GO OLD-SCHOOL, CORNMEAL.
- SEASONINGS—OLD BAY, GROUND PEPPER AND SALT, PAPRIKA, A HANDFUL OF LEMONS (2 TO 3) FOR SQUEEZING.
- BLEND OF SOYBEAN AND PEANUT OIL, IF YOU CAN FIND IT. IF NOT, VEGETABLE OIL WILL DO JUST FINE.
- LARGE SKILLET, FRYDADDY, OR ELECTRIC FRYER. (OR, ONE OF THOSE BIG OL' FISH COOKERS. I'D RATHER YOU NOT, THOUGH. LIKE SONG NUMBER TEN ON THE EAGLES EPIC ALBUM *HOTEL CALIFORNIA*, USING A FISH COOKER TO FRY FISH OF ANY KIND IS THE LAST RESORT. UNLESS YOU REALLY *ARE* FEEDING THE 5,000.)
- PROPER SET OF TONGS OR STRAINING SPOON.
- PAPER-TOWELED PLATES.

PREPARATION

Take a couple dressed fish (told you we were going dancing) from the bucket and drop them into the deep pan or pot full of breading. Season with Old Bay, ground pepper, salt, paprika, and, if you like, a squeeze or two of lemon. Flippity-flop the fish around till they're good and coated. Once the oil in your FryDaddy or skillet is sufficiently hot, *gently* slide in the fish. You should hear a nice crackling sound, like amplified Rice Krispies.

Take your straining spoon and get ready to stir. Not like you would a pot of soup but a pot of dumplings—more pushing instead of swirling.

After a few minutes, you should see the fish floating on top of the oil, making one last swim to greatness.

Scoop out the fish and place on a paper-toweled plate. Dab gently with another paper towel. Wait for a minute, two at the most. If not too hot, with your thumb, middle and forefinger, jiggle out the dorsal fin. Sometimes it slides right out, sometimes not. If not, that's OK. Just take your fork and flake off a few nice pulls of meat. Squeeze a little lemon on these prize possessions, pop a bite in your mouth, and chew slowly. Savor the flavor of perfectly cooked fish. Pat yourself on the back.

You deserve it.

POMPANO AND CIRCUMSTANCE

I t's hard to beat fresh fried bream no matter how many sticks you use, but when Freddie pan-fried pompano it came pretty darn close.

If you're not a big fish person, finding yourself turned off by the lingering fishy taste some of these swimmers leave behind, give pompano a try. Indigenous to the warm waters of the Atlantic, pompano, like the rest of us, love the Florida coast.

A lovely, meaty fish, pompano are easy to eat and mild as Clark Kent. As a young lad I was treated to this delicacy many times in my parents' kitchen, thanks to Freddie Bennett's culinary skills and the generosity of Chef James "Bollie" Clark, Augusta National's head chef for almost 30 years.

There's no doubt in my mind Freddie's pan-fried pompano lit the fire for my love of anything saltwater, a fire that still burns Roman candle bright some forty years later. While the pompano you're frying at home may not be as fresh as the pompano I was fortunate to know (Freddie's pompano was often pan-fried less than 24 hours from the last time it dipped its toes in the Atlantic), I promise you are in for one heck of a tasty treat, and so are your guests!

POMPANO

(SERVES 4-6)

INGREDIENTS AND TOOLS OF THE TRADE

- APRON. BUT ONLY IF YOU ARE CONCERNED ABOUT GREASE STAINS ON YOUR CLOTHES THAT STAY WITH YOU LIKE A BIRTHMARK.
- BORDEN OR LAND O'LAKES HALF-AND-HALF CREAM.
- DECENT-SIZED BOWL FOR DIPPING THE POMPANO INTO THE HALF-AND-HALF.
- 4–6 PIECES OF FRESH POMPANO FILLETS. IF YOU CAN'T FIND POMPANO, TILAPIA OR FLOUNDER WILL DO JUST FINE, AS WILL SEA BASS, BUT BE FOREWARNED THAT THE FOLKS RINGING UP SEA BASS ARE DAMN PROUD OF IT. IF THEY SAY IT'S CHILEAN, AND YOU AIN'T IN CHILE, RUN AWAY, FAST AS YOU CAN.
- A GOOD-SIZED PAN TO SEASON AND BREAD THE FISH.
- SALT, OR SEA SALT, IF YOU LIKE (FREDDIE ALWAYS USED MORTON'S).
- GROUND PEPPER.
- HOUSE-AUTRY SEAFOOD BREADING.
- LEMONS FOR SQUEEZING WHILE COOKING AND EATING.
- OLIVE OIL.
- PROPER SKILLET. HOPEFULLY, YOU HAVE ONE BY NOW. IF NOT, I'LL WAIT HERE TILL YOU GET ONE.
- TONGS. LONG ENOUGH THAT YOU DON'T GET BURNED.
- GAS BURNERS. AN ELECTRIC STOVE EYE WILL DO, BUT SO WILL A TOP-FLIGHT XL IF YOU'RE OUT OF PROVIS. (I'M KIDDING—SORT OF. SOME ELECTRIC EYES ARE BETTER THAN OTHERS.)
- HOMEMADE TARTAR SAUCE (SEE ONE HECK OF A RECIPE UNDER CLUBHOUSE CRAB CAKES, PAGE 77).

25

PREPARATION

Don that apron. It looks good on you.

Pour the half-and-half into the bowl. Take each piece of pompano and submerge into the creamy goodness. After a good soaking, remove the fish and place in the good-sized pan for seasoning and breading. Season with salt and pepper. Here's where your practiced art of dashing, prancing, and vixening come in handy.

Shake on the House-Autry breading, giving the pompano a nice, thin coating. (Think gliding on lipstick, not caulking a tub.) Squeeze on fresh lemon juice—how much is up to you. Hang tight, and turn your attention to that proper skillet.

Poor in some oil, about a knuckle deep, then turn the front burner to medium, so you can be as close to the action as possible. When the oil starts to bubble (think carbonation, not gum) take the tongs and slide a few pieces of fish into the skillet, like you're sliding feet first into home with no chance of getting out. Listen for the sizzle, the crackle, the occasional pop. The sooner you learn the meaning of these sounds, the sooner you'll be able to differentiate when the oil is saying cook a little longer versus flip it over right now, and the better cook you will be.

Flip the pompano when you think it's time. Don't use a timer, unless it's in your head. *Now* is the time for trial—the error may or may not be.

When the pompano turns brown as a peanut, it's time to depart the oily waters of your skillet for dryer land—the paper towel-lined plate. Spread the fish out best you can as you lay them out. Room to breathe is a very good thing.

Take your clean fingers (yes, your fingers—assuming you washed them when you washed your hands) and break off a piece of pompano. The outer edge of the fish should be the color of east coast beach sand before the tide comes in; the inside should be white and flaky, but not like snow—more like if you were peeling back the layers of a sweet onion.

If you like lemon as much as I do, now's the time to drizzle a little juice on that Pompano goodness. If you're anything like the princess in *Princess and the Pea* when it comes to seeds, you might want to slip one of those little hair nets on your lemon halves.

Take a bite of that perfectly cooked fish. You've earned it. If it tastes as good as I know it will, fry up the remaining pieces and serve immediately while hot.

Cold chicken still works, but cold fish is out of a job.

THE LOST ART OF BUTTER BEANS

If he were alive today, iconic Augusta National caddy master Freddie Bennett would shake his head at me for describing him as such, humbly preferring he be remembered as an everyman, a friend to everyone, a loving husband and beloved daddy. And that's so true; he was. But "iconic" fits, too. No one knew the ins and outs of Augusta National like Freddie Bennett, before or since. He ruled our caddy world with an iron fist wrapped in velvet, owned the quickest wit I've ever witnessed, had a memory that shames computers, and on mornings when the previous evening's stars aligned and the mood was right, Freddie had a gift for making gastronomical magic out of everything he touched. But of all the dishes Freddie dialed up and doled out from the caddy house kitchen, his breakfast butter beans knew no peer.

You can scrunch your nose all you want at the thought of legumes before lunch (fair enough—they were long gone by lunchtime anyway), but once you master this recipe, I *promise* you'll think differently about butter beans, and when to serve up this veritable vegetable.

What follows is this timeless dish, as best I remember it.

FREDDIE BENNETT'S BUTTER BEANS

(FEEDS 12-14)

INGREDIENTS AND TOOLS OF THE TRADE

- Nonstick cooking spray. I like the grill-worthy kind.
- Big ol' pot, at least 7 quarts. I love my Le Creuset. They ain't cheap, but how many things that last a lifetime are?
- HoneyBaked ham bone, but if you don't have HoneyBaked, a good, meaty ham bone works just fine.
- Sizeable plate for placing said ham bone after you boil it on up (also for collecting prized ham juices).
- 1 32-ounce box Kitchen Basics chicken stock.
- Ground pepper.
- Pepper vinegar.
- Red wine vinegar.
- Agave, or honey—I'm cool with either, though I prefer agave if you have some. It's as natural as a Southern guilt trip!
- Goya powdered chicken bouillon.
- A stirring spoon with a handle long enough for you to stir the pot without burning the skin off your fingers.
- Large Ziploc bag or grocery bag for placing over the ham to trap in steamed flavor. This is key.
- A stick of proper butter, like Kerrygold or Olivio.

- Three 24-ounce bags of frozen butter beans, also known as fordhook, baby limas, *Phaseolus Lunatus*, or runner beans, depending on what circles you run in. But let's just call 'em "butter beans."
- A long-handled ladle (see above as to why the long handle).
- Makings for perfect pot liquor (see recipe for Perfect Pot Liquor, page 13)

PREPARATION

Spray your pot with cooking spray—this is as much prevent defense as it is anything. Fill that pot about 1/3 full of water and *carefully* slide in the ham bone—this ain't Splash Mountain. The meatier the ham bone the better. Turn on your favorite burner, pour in the whole carton of chicken stock, and dash in some ground pepper, red wine vinegar, and a little pepper vinegar. Squeeze in a bit of agave, even if you were lucky enough to score a HoneyBaked Ham bone. Add a pack of chicken Goya.

Bring it all to a rolling boil, but don't cover. Boiling water, unlike drying paint, is fun to watch, especially when it's full of butter beans and ham. Let the excitement go on for about 30–45 minutes or so until you are fairly convinced the ham meat can be pulled off the bone with little to no effort on your part. Save your strength for later.

Turn down the burner.

Take the ham bone from the pot and put it on a sizeable plate, one that can easily hold the juices without spilling them all over the floor. These juices will come in handy later.

Cover the ham bone with a gallon Ziploc bag or plastic grocery bag. The key here is keeping the ham bone moist while you wait for it to cool. Don't be fooled—boiled ham will burn the shit out of you.

Turn the burner back up.

Cut off a couple slabs of real butter and add to the mix. Get the water boiling again and pour in all the butter beans. Fine if they've thawed out a little—like your in-laws after a couple uneventful Christmas dinners. (But not *my* in-laws. Mine are pretty cool.)

Stir the butter beans to make sure they're separated—like the couple who didn't fare quite as well with their in-laws' Christmas dinners. On a more serious note, frozen butter beans can sometimes form into little green snowballs, so be sure to give the ol' pot at least one good swirl of the stirring spoon. With that same spoon, better yet a ladle if you have one, scoop out a wee dram of the pot liquor. I doubt it's ready for prime time, but now is a *great* time to see how far along on the road to perfect pot liquor you really are. OK, think for me: what's it need? What's it calling for? A splash of red wine vinegar? Pepper vinegar? A little garlic salt?

The only way to find out is to, well, find out.

Work your magic on the pot liquor, remembering the "debunking the myth" recipe, and cut the heat to where the water and butter beans are gently lolling (not rolling), looking like green lava foam from your favorite sci fi movie!

Give it 15–20 minutes, covered or uncovered. Your call.

Time to taste the goods—the pot liquor, not the butter beans. Butter beans will need to go a little longer—say another 30 minutes or so. Though, in my mind, you can't really cook 'em too long.

So, how's the pot liquor? Pretty darn good, I bet. But if it needs a touch of this or a pinch of that, go right ahead. This is your baby, not mine. It's you they'll be looking at across the table, not me.

Make 'em smile!

Last step: The ham bone. Is it cool to the touch? Room temperature? (Never understood that one, truth be told. What if my room is hotter than yours?) If the answer is yes, pull those decadent hunks of ham from the bone, careful to rid the meat of any unwanted fat or gristle. Add those lovely ham bits to the pot—shredding them by hand if you like. I like 'em about thumb size, and irregular in shape. But for the love of all that is holy, no blocks.

This ain't a romper room.

Take a moment and give all the ingredients a good stirring up, like a high school rumor mill. Turn down the heat and smell the simmering goodness. Has it been an hour yet? Don't look at me—you're the one with the timer, and it better be in your head. If it has, you're close. Might even be close enough to know where you've arrived: Butter Bean Heaven. Or as Mr. Krabs once said to SpongeBob when SpongeBob finally mastered the order of pickles, patty, mustard, and bun, "Me boy... It's *time*."

If so, pull your favorite spoon from the drawer—I know you have one. Maybe it's monogrammed with letters other than your own; maybe it's tarnished hotel silverware bought from an antique vendor at a coastal flea market, or maybe you pocketed it from the local eatery after too many fizzy lifting drinks. Maybe it's your favorite spoon for reasons known only to you.

Got it? Good. Spoon up some of that pot liquor goodness and close your eyes as you take the smallest of sips. If that small sip makes for a big smile, then my work here is done.

Well, almost.

Spoon up some butter beans. I'm not going to tell you how they should taste, or lecture about texture. In fact, I'm not even going to ask. But I gotta know one small thing: Do they make you smile? Off the record, squishy white bread goes great with grins.

Dip away.

AND NOW, A WORD FROM OUR SPONSORS

Well, there aren't any.

Like the great Bobby Jones, who many consider to be the best to ever play the game, who played equipment he loved and believed in not because he was paid to do so but because he felt they gave him the best chance to be the absolute best, so go I. When I'm cooking, I use what I use because I like the way it tastes, the way it enhances a dish, the way it takes my cooking and me to another level, a level I could never get to on my own. I'm not a big fan of heights, but I gotta admit I like what I see when I'm up here.

How 'bout I show you around?

FAVORITE INGREDIENTS AND TOOLS OF THE TRADE

- Goya powdered bullion—chicken and ham
- Baker's Select basil leaves
- McCormick lemon pepper with parsley
- Kirkland coarse ground Malabar black pepper
- Ground black pepper in general
- McCormick celery salt
- McCormick Mediterranean blend garlic salt
- Old Bay Seasoning
- Spice World paprika
- Organic milk
- Bay leaves—any brand will do. These babies have been hanging around kitchens since the dawn of time.
- Welch's 100% grape juice

- Schweppes ginger ale
- Gruet blanc de noirs methode champenoise
- HoneyBaked Ham bones and pieces
- Southern Home butter beans
- Southern Home frozen okra
- Colonial King Thin bread
- Nature's Own Perfectly Crafted white or whole grain bread
- Eggland's Best eggs
- Heinz Tomato Ketchup
- Plochman's mild yellow mustard
- Kerrygold Pure Irish Butter
- Hillshire Farm kielbasa
- Bush's Best beans
- "Darn Good" chili soup mix
- Stubb's BBQ sauces and marinades
- Duke's Mayonnaise
- Kitchen Basics Original Chicken Stock
- Kirkland organic chicken stock
- Blue agave
- Morton table salt
- Himalayan pink sea salt
- Wondra quick-mixing flour: enriched, bleached, all-purpose
- White Lily flour
- House-Autry breading, be it chicken, pork, or seafood
- Texas Pete hot sauce
- Frank's RedHot sauce
- Texas Pete pepper vinegar
- Newman's Own Sockarooni spaghetti sauce
- Newman's Own anything and everything
- Lea & Perrins Worcestershire sauce
- La Choy soy sauce. You want a soy sauce that complements, not overwhelms.
- Kikkoman soy sauce, if you can't find La Choy.
- Del Monte stewed or diced tomatoes
- Pompeii red wine vinegar
- Pompeii lemon juice, lime juice
- Old El Paso taco seasoning
- Frontera skillet sauce, both taco and fajita
- Pure olive oil, but stay away from extra virgin unless you really want to taste it
- Bertolli olive oil spray
- Gas stove
- Gas oven
- FryDaddy, Fry Grandpappy
- Electric fryer
- Electric skillet
- All things Le Creuset: Dutch ovens, pots, pans, skillets, utensils, hot pads
- KitchenGrips—as many as you can get your hands on
- Henkel knives
- If not Henkel, proper, sharp knives that can be sharpened again and again
- Metal whisk—one that looks like a horseshoe Slinky at the base
- Long-handled slotted stirring/serving spoon
- Calphalon metal tongs
- I'm sure I've missed a few—this is quite the surface to scratch! Add to the list with your own favorites.

FROM JUST OUTSIDE AUGUSTA, I BRING YOU MISS LILLIE

Collard greens are as southern as a handshake deal. Lillie always called them greens, whether they were collard, mustard, or turnip.

I called them amazing.

Having lived the majority of her devoutly Christian life just a par 5 and change away from Augusta National, Miss Lillie May Winfield knew enough about that gated world to know she could not care less about it. Her love was the Lord, family, her dogs, and believe it or not, me. Lillie called the Sand Hills community home, the very same neighborhood so many of Augusta's finest caddies spent their off-course hours playing cards, spinning stories, and blowing through a day's wages like Tasmanian devils on the take. It was not unusual for a caddy worth his salt to stroll out of Augusta's iron gates with $200 cash in his pockets, only to show up the next morning with two empties. I often wondered where the money went, even at times when I saw it fly out the proverbial window like dandelions in a March wind, having been on the giving end of that flight once or twice myself.

Miss Lillie took care of my family for over twenty-five years of Fridays, though to call her our maid would be like calling Shakespeare a writer. She was so much more than that. Miss Lillie—I called her Lil—was more like a favorite aunt to me; the aunt who knew all my secrets, both trade and best kept, along with every skeleton in my closet, especially the ones that rattled around during my teenage years. Or any year, for that matter.

Lucky for us, before Lil left her earthly body for a heavenly one, she left me the recipe for her collard greens.

She lives on in every batch I make.

Before we get to making greens, I gotta come clean. During my Augusta caddy days, I tried my hand a time or two at making this untouchable dish, only to miss not just the boat, but the dock and the slip, too. Try as I might, I could never get my greens as tender (or tasty) as Lil's. Hers were tender as baby spinach; mine were 3X5 index cards with last month's grocery list scribbled in indelible ink. Fifteen years (and holy matrimony—at least I got one thing right) would pass before I tried again.

If the third time's a charm, this was the whole bracelet.

I wish I could say exactly where I was when it hit me, like people can say exactly where they were when Elvis died, Skynyrd crashed, Michael Jackson moonwalked for the very first time. But I can't. I *can* remember, however, exactly *what* I was doing. I was holding Lil's collard greens recipe in my still untrained hand, looking at it with my equally untrained eye, and that's when I saw it, as obvious as an ice-cold whiff.

Don't (pause) drown 'em (pause), Tripp.

The handwriting was mine, but the voice was Lil's. *Don't drown your greens, darlin'.* Her laywoman's way of simply saying: sauté. And that's exactly what we're going to do.

But before we fly off into that collard green sunset, first we gotta gas up the plane. For the record, the hand you're holding isn't mine.

It's Lil's.

MISS LILLIE WINFIELD'S CADDY YARD COLLARDS

(FEEDS 12-16)

INGREDIENTS AND TOOLS OF THE TRADE FOR THE BEST COLLARD GREENS THIS SIDE OF THE PEARLY GATES (AND MAYBE THE OTHER SIDE, TOO)

- 7–8 BATCHES OF WASHED AND RUBBER-BANDED COLLARD GREENS. THAT'S A LOT, I KNOW, BUT WHETHER YOU FEED ONE CUSTOMER OR 100, YOU STILL GOTTA BUILD THE RESTAURANT. MIGHT AS WELL BUILD A GOOD ONE.
- PROPER PAIR OF KITCHEN SCISSORS, AND I DON'T MEAN THE KIND YOU GET AT DOLLAR GENERAL.
- BIG OL' POT FOR BOILING THE HAM UNTIL THE MEAT FALLS OFF THE BONE.
- HONEYBAKED HAM BONE. (LIL ALSO WARNED, "NO SMOKED MEAT.")
- HONEYBAKED HAM PIECES, IF YOU CAN FIND THEM—IT'S OK IF YOU CAN'T.
- 2 PACKETS OF GOYA CHICKEN BOUILLON.
- MEDITERRANEAN BLEND GARLIC SALT.
- LEMON PEPPER.
- GROUND PEPPER.
- CELERY SALT.
- KITCHEN BASICS CHICKEN STOCK—A LOT MORE PROTEIN, A LOT MORE TASTE, AND 1/3 LESS SALT THAN THE OTHER BRANDS.
- SPLENDA, OR ANY POWDERED SWEETENER THAT WILL LAY THE WOOD TO A WHITE MOUSE IF HE EATS 6,000 POUNDS OF THE POWDERY STUFF IN ONE SITTING!
- BLUE AGAVE SWEETENER.

- R ED WINE VINEGAR.
- G OOD-SIZED BOWL TO PUT THE TRIMMED COLLARDS.
- T ASTING SPOON (GOTTA TASTE IT AS YOU GO ALONG).
- P EPPER VINEGAR (OPTIONAL).
- P ATIENCE, BUT NOT OF J OB. M ORE LIKE THE KIND YOU NEED FOR FISHING.

Shall we begin? It's a process, sure, but so is falling in love, even when it's at first sight. There is so much more to see than you realize.

PREPARATION

Collards worth cooking are always a deep, endless green color, with no yellowing and no grit. Don't be afraid to rub the inside of each batch with your fingers and lick 'em when no one's looking. Or show some confidence and lick 'em when they are. That's the *only* way to tell for sure if those collards have been thoroughly cleaned. The old adage about putting greens in the washing machine to clean them? Shiiit.

That's like trying to wash sand off the beach!

Find a comfortable spot at the kitchen table and set up shop with a good-sized bowl and your favorite pair of kitchen scissors. We're cutting these collards off of their stems, not tearing them. The only thing I want you tearing is the page out of any cookbook that says rip the collard leaves into bite-sized pieces. Remember the classic scene in *Dead Poets Society*, when Robin Williams instructs his English class to tear out page 21 of *Understanding Poetry* by J. Evans Pritchard, PhD?

That's exactly what we're doing here.

Now, take your scissors and cut the rubber bands off each bunch of collards. Watch as the stalks and stems expand out like butterfly wings, swallows bound for Capistrano, or in this case your big ol' pot with just the right amount of water and seasonings boiling on the stove. You know, the pot with the HoneyBaked ham bone and the pre-liquor pot liquor. I know, I know. I haven't told you that step yet.

All in good time, my friend.

Go get the biggest pot you own, unless you're from New Orleans and you make your living boiling crawfish. In that case, get the *second* biggest pot you own. I always use my

grandfather's, a Sears and Roebuck 12-quart aluminum special Papa bought with leftover money from his first paycheck as a security guard at the Sears on the corner of Peachtree and North Avenue, just a driver/wedge from the Georgia Institute of Technology, where Bobby Jones went to college.

Fill your pot about 1/3 full of water; *hot* water, if you want it to boil faster. (Joke's on you, typical cookbooks.) Ease in the HoneyBaked ham bone, and a couple packs of chicken Goya with a dash or two of the garlic salt, lemon pepper, ground pepper, celery salt, the whole shootin' match of Kitchen Basics chicken stock, a pack of powdered sweetener and a few squeezes of agave. Whew. Splash in a little red wine vinegar, crank up the heat like the volume on the ol' turntable, and return to the plethora of collards in dire need of your scissorly ways. Commence to cutting.

Best way is your way, whatever way that is.

What I like to do is break off each stalk at the base, cutting the collard leaves from bottom to top, right side then left. Let the long leaves fall into that big ol' bowl I asked you to grab earlier. Do this for at least one entire bunch. I usually do it for two, or until the bowl is brimming with collards, as stuffed as a feather pillow. Now, go back and cut the long leaves into manageable strips—remember the index cards? But this time that's a good thing. And when I say cut, I mean cut with scissors. No tearing, unless you're still working on that page in the other cookbook.

We want clean cuts, because clean cuts mean tender greens. Fifteen will get you twenty, and tearing your greens will make them tougher than a Dollar Store ribeye!

By now (you should be about 1/2 an hour in), the pot with our HoneyBaked ham bone friend should be boiling like a kettle and filling your kitchen with pot liquor perfume. You can take the ham bone out now if you'd like; I prefer to leave it in as long as life will let me. Add the cut greens—whole bowl if you can—then push 'em down and stir 'em 'round like a rumor mill, except here we ain't cooking up nothing but the truth!

This is what I mean by sautéing your greens. *Don't drown 'em.* You want them treading water, knowing damn good and well they could stand up if they wanted to.

Turn the heat down just a little, so the boiling turns to bubbling, and repeat the steps where you cut that batch or two of collards. Always off the stem, right side, left side. Long leaves, then manageable strips. Once your bowl is full, toss the neatly trimmed greens into the pot in progress and press down and stir. Stir, and press down. See the leaves wilt like Chicken Little? Well, now you know what to look for. Let your sense of smell kick in, earn its wages. What do you smell right now? Do you need to add a little more agave? Red wine vinegar? Maybe micro up another batch of pre-liquor pot liquor? Need to add a dash or two more of ground pepper vinegar?

This is where the coach puts his whistle in the ol' spandex back pocket, crosses his arms like he's deep in thought, and shuts the hell up. This is where *you* shine, and my diamonds go back in the box.

Engage, Maverick.

For those taking notes, I've waited half my life to see those two words side by side in print.

For those *not* taking notes, go spoon up some generous bowls of the best tasting collard greens this side of the Pearly Gates. Your guests are waiting. If you've cooked these greens right—and I'll bet you have—your guests are about to become family.

Welcome home.

COLLARD GREENS:
A SOUP FOR ALL SEASONS

Folks who say soup is a wintertime food have never had this one. Once you've gone through the labor of love to properly make collards, taking the soup step is as easy as tapping in for a double bogey 6 to miss the cut by five.

That one's good, old sock. Pick it up.

To make this magical, brothy dish, there are two ways you can go. The first is simple as a shoelace. Just add a little extra pot liquor (the kind you learned to make a few recipes back and now you own it), and a handful or three of HoneyBaked ham chunks, or pieces, if you were able to score some, though almost any nice ham chunks will do.

If you want to go all out—why not, you're dressed for it—go get another HoneyBaked ham bone and follow the ham bone steps when you first made your collard greens. Don't be afraid to rolling boil that ham bone into oblivion. The meat you want for collard greens soup is closest to the bone and when it's ready, pulling it off the bone will be like picking apples off a tree.

The second road that leads to this some kinda good collard greens soup has a few more twists and turns, but you'll find it no less scenic than the first.

Take a picture, if you like.

CADDY YARD COLLARD GREENS SOUP

(SERVES 12-16)

INGREDIENTS AND TOOLS OF THE TRADE

- GOOD-SIZED POT. SEVEN QUARTS OR HIGHER.
- YOUR ALREADY-MADE, BY *YOUR* HANDS, COLLARD GREENS, HAM SLIVERS, AND POT LIQUOR AU JUS.
- OPTION 1: A COUPLE 16-OUNCE PACKAGES OF GROUND SAUSAGE, SUCH AS JIMMY DEAN BREAKFAST SAUSAGE. STAY AWAY FROM CUTE FLAVORS HERE LIKE MAPLE OR SAGE. SAVE THOSE FOR THE BISCUITS.
- OPTION 2: GO BRAT STYLE: ITALIAN, BEER, OR MILD SAUSAGE—THE KIND WITH CASINGS. I'M QUITE COOL WITH EITHER GROUND OR BRAT. THEY BOTH WORK JUST FINE.
- SPATULA—I PREFER METAL FOR BROWNING SAUSAGE. DON'T WORRY, YOU WON'T HARM YOUR NONSTICK PAN. *THAT* IS A MARKETING MYTH.
- NONSTICK SKILLET (THE KIND YOU CAN'T HARM)—BRAND MATTERS HERE IF YOU WANT LONGEVITY, AND YOU KNOW I LOVE ME SOME CALPHALON! STILL GOT THE POTS AND PANS FROM OUR WEDDING OVER TWENTY YEARS AGO, IN FACT. AND I USE 'EM EVERY DAY.
- THE USUAL SUSPECTS OF SEASONING FOR BROWNING ANY MEAT: SOY SAUCE, WORCESTERSHIRE, LEMON JUICE, CELERY SALT, GARLIC SALT, LEMON PEPPER, GROUND PEPPER, BUT THIS TIME ADD A SPLASH OF PEPPER VINEGAR. ADD *TWO* SPLASHES, IF YOU THINK IT NEEDS IT.
- SLOTTED LONG-HANDLED STRAINER SPOON, OR JUST A LONG-HANDLED STRAINER SPOON. THE STRAIN IN SPAIN FALLS MAINLY BACK IN THE PAN.

- PROPER KITCHEN SCISSORS. SOME CHEFS CALL THEM SHEARS—THOSE SAME CHEFS ALSO HAVE SHEEP OUT BACK, SO WATCH YOURS!
- TWO 32-OUNCE BOXES OF KITCHEN BASICS CHICKEN STOCK.

PREPARATION

The next few steps are easy like Sunday morning.

From your pot of perfect collards, cull (man, that's a great word) as much greens, ham slivers, and pot liquor as you like and add them to your soup pot. Ham and sausage soaking in the same swimming hole may sound like Hatfield and McCoy, but in here they're coffee and crullers.

If you're going with ground sausage (brat-style method to follow), brown the meat same as you would ground beef. Sausage is a different consistency than beef, of course, but you can Edwin Moses that hurdle with ease simply by using any edge of your spatula (metal spatulas rock like a hurricane for this task) to knife your way through the sausage, flipping and turning the meat as it browns. The result will be slightly larger chunks, but when you taste them you'll wish they were even bigger!

When the sausage is good and done, it'll be firm with a bit of flex, like a tight ab muscle (were mine ever like that?). Use that slotted strainer spoon to scoop the sausage into the soup pot of collard greens, ham, and pot liquor. Resist the urge to drain the meat. A little sausage au jus is a wonderful thing (like Tigger) and will send this soup into the stratosphere with your taste buds taking the Gs like Chase and Aykroyd in *Spies Like Us*.

If you'd like to try brat-style sausage—as always, the choice is yours—make sure you separate the sausage from its casing (otherwise, grab a bun and grill some peppers). This is easy when you use that proper pair of kitchen scissors I told you to get. Just cut the casing down the middle and ease out the sausage, breaking it up with your fingers before putting it into the skillet to brown. Season and stir with your slotted spoon just like you did with the ground sausage. When it's brown as a brick, scoop the meat into the soup pot of collards and ham, resisting the urge to drain, unless you're unclogging conventional ways of thinking.

Remember: sausage au jus is a beautiful thing.

With all your goodies in the pot, add the chicken stock and any more seasonings you deem fit. I'm a big fan of broth, so I pour in the whole container(s). With the burner on medium, stir one last time and let the soup get as happy as a forest of Bob Ross trees!

Serve with cornbread, if you like (you're on your own for that recipe—I can barely work an Easy-Bake Oven). Me, I like my collard greens soup straight up, eaten from a favorite coffee mug with the biggest soup spoon I can find.

How about you?

THE KITCHEN IN THE CLUBHOUSE

Though he trained under some of the world's finest chefs and quietly honed his craft within watchful eyes of culinary legends from as far away as Germany and France, Chef James Clark was a country boy at heart, with Carolina blood in his veins. A meat and potatoes kind of cook, Chef Clark's idea of the perfect meal was a quick 9 holes at Augusta before firing up commercial-grade ovens, whipping up a little this and a little that, seeing the smiles on the faces of Augusta's members and guests when the oven smoke cleared, and heading for the barn.

Mornings come very early at Augusta National.

But all that changed when an Augusta member placed an order for pound cake. A founding member, of all things. The chairman, in fact. Why, it was none other than Mr. Clifford Roberts, the very man who, along with legendary Bobby Jones, created (during the Great Depression, I might add) what would one day become the most exclusive and coveted golf club in all the world.

But for tonight, this ol' golf club was in bad need of a recipe for pound cake.

In town from a New York business trip with a few gentlemen who'd done a mighty fine job on a business merger that nicely padded the pockets of both Mr. Roberts and his dinner guests, Augusta's chairman was eager to show off his revered golf club, and in particular his newest hire, Chef James Clark. Mr. Cliff had handpicked Chef from the highly respected Breakers Resort in Palm Beach, Florida, on the subtly strong suggestion of a trusted advisor who also happened to be an Augusta member.

Fast forward a few clicks of the clock.

As cocktails quickly arrive, Mr. Roberts calls Chef over and tells him in no uncertain terms he knows exactly what he would like for dinner. What they would *all* like for dinner.

"Yes, sir, Mr. Roberts. Now, what might that be? What can I cook up for you and your guests this fine evening?"

Mr. Roberts mulls the thought over and over, with chin in hand before finally speaking. "Well, Chef, it is indeed a fine evening . . . and I think I'd like some roasted lamb, though not too well done, with grilled potatoes on the side. *Small* potatoes, you see. Again, not too well done. And a nice bottle of port, perhaps, unless you would like to recommend a wine that might better complement such a fine meal?"

Chef, who never drank anything stronger than water, nods and says, "I'll send Frank Carpenter right over, Mr. Roberts. He knows far better than me about what wine goes with what."

Chef is right as rain on that bit of insight, as Frank Carpenter will proudly wear the sommelier badge of honor at Augusta National for over 40 years, holding court over what is considered by those in the know to be the finest collection of wine and spirits in the world.

Working his way back to the kitchen, Chef runs Mr. Roberts's meal request through his mental Rolodex and quickly deduces—quite accurately—that his new boss has simply asked for a meat and potatoes kind of meal, a request right up Chef's alley!

"Yes, sir, Mr. Roberts," says Chef, whispering under his breath: *I'm on it. Man, am I ever on it.* But before Chef can slide through the swinging doors, Mr. Roberts calls out his name.

"Uhhh, one more thing, please, Chef."

"Yes, sir?"

"Well, you see, as I mentioned earlier, these boys here have done a mighty fine job for me, recently, and I've been telling them how we have the best of everything here at Augusta, and well, I just know that the best of everything has to include my favorite dessert. I would like to order that, to finish out our meal tonight."

"Yes, sir, Mr. Roberts. Sure thing." Chef waits for the other shoe to drop, but it never does. "And what might that be, Mr. Roberts? Your favorite dessert, I mean."

"Pound cake, Chef. What other dessert is there?"

Chef's jaw drops like it's tied to a boat anchor.

"Oh, yes sir, Mr. Roberts. Pound cake. You got it. Yes, sir. Pound cake. I'm on it."

Well, Chef wasn't on shit.

Chef didn't know crème brûlée from a cream-filled doughnut; desserts and baking were simply not in his wheelhouse, not *this* wheelhouse, anyway. But he *did* know Kroger, the all-night grocery across the street from Augusta National.

Like a stealth bomber dressed in all white cooking garb, Chef slips across the street to the Kroger, picks up a few tins of Sara Lee pound cake, sneaks back to the kitchen, warms up the tins and lightly toasts the slices, and presents them to Mr. Roberts as Chef Clark's Augusta National secret recipe pound cake. Breathing a sigh of relief, Chef grins like the Pink Panther and heads back through the swinging doors of his kitchen.

It's important to note here that Clifford Roberts wasn't like the rest of us in that he seldom did his own shopping, rarely ever set foot in a grocery store, and wouldn't know Sara Lee if she walked up and bit him on the ass!

"Well, didn't I tell you boys? Didn't I tell you?" says Mr. Roberts, knifing into his pound cake a proud and confident man. "Did I not tell you Augusta National has the best of everything there is to offer?"

A chorus of yessirs follows Chef to the almost swinging open doors, before another voice stops him once again.

"Chef?"

"Yes, sir, Mr. Roberts?"

"Chef, I want to thank you for a wonderful meal tonight. You outdid yourself. Just simply outdid yourself. But there *is* one thing before you go. I know it's getting late, and morning comes early around here."

"Yes, sir?"

"I'd like the recipe."

"The recipe for what, sir?"

"The pound cake."

Oh, shit.

For the rest of the season, Chef Clark does his best to duck Mr. Roberts when it comes to asking Chef for the elusive, secret pound cake recipe. When the golf season at Augusta mercifully ends (for Chef) the third week in May, Mr. Roberts, a bit fed up but rabbit-anxious to head home to cooler weather and fewer headaches, confronts Chef Clark in the kitchen and demands to be heard.

"Chef, I don't know why you've been avoiding me all season long and I don't have the time right now to find out why. All I want is that damn pound cake recipe so I can take it home to New York, give it to my private chef, and he can make it for me and the wife. She has a bit of the sweet tooth as well, you see, and a recipe like this would go far in helping me get back in good graces, what with me being gone all the time."

Speaking of gone, Chef wishes he was, too.

With nowhere to run and nowhere to hide, Chef has no choice but to give up the ghost.

"It's Sara Lee, sir."

"What?"

"The pound cake, sir. It's Sara Lee."

Long pause.

"What?"

"Mr. Roberts, the pound cake. It's, it's

Sara Lee." Chef stares a hole in the kitchen floor too small to crawl into, looks up. His words come out slow as syrup. "Sir, that pound cake is *Sara Lee.*"

"Chef, I don't give a damn if it's *Robert* E. Lee! I-want-that-recipe!"

An untimely death took Chef James Clark from us far too early, but for as long as he was alive, the Augusta National secret recipe for pound cake was Sara Lee.

CHEF CLARK'S SECRET RECIPE AUGUSTA NATIONAL POUND CAKE, WITH A NOD TO SARA LEE

(SERVES 6-8)

INGREDIENTS AND TOOLS OF THE TRADE

- 1 Sara Lee Family Size All Butter Pound Cake.
- 1 oven or toaster you can discreetly turn on.
- The ability to slip out to the nearest grocery store undetected and pick up a tin or two of Sara Lee products.
- A mighty sharp knife for slicing the pound cake.
- Proper butter that's as easy to spread as a high school rumor, such as Olivio, Kerrygold, or Land O'Lakes.
- Forks for each guest.
- Plates to match.
- Nice tray for serving (I bet you have one from your wedding registry or hidden in the back of your cupboard—now's the time to put it to good use!).
- The gift for keeping a straight face when guests praise your baking abilities.
- The wherewithal to tell them the truth behind the recipe.

PREPARATION

Turn your oven to 375. No need to preheat, this baby's already fully cooked, and (hopefully) for the most part, thawed out. You can either leave Sara in the tin for a moister crust or remove and place on baking sheet for a crispier one—up to you. Either way, pop that tin in

53

the oven for 15–20 minutes, or until she's a little browner than she was when you bought her. Remove and place on a cutting board to cool for a few minutes. Just cool enough to touch, since you are going to slice it and therefore touch it with your hands, but still warm enough to melt just the slightest smidge of butter.

With that sharp knife, cut the pound cake into slices about the thickness of a small stack of bills—mail, not dollars. If you want to go all out, pop the slices back into the oven a few minutes for that little extra golden-brown touch that's sure to make this dish appear even more homemade. Add the slightest dollop of butter to each slice, making sure at least a crest of the butter is visible. We're riding the illusional wave here, my friend.

Serve (while still warm) on those plates I asked you to gather. Put those glistening forks on the plates so they're touching the pound cake slices.

Food touching cutlery.

Doesn't get much more down-home than that.

PANCHO AND LEFTY

In most restaurants, especially the budget-breakers, à la carte means extra eats at extra costs. Here in *The Caddy's Cookbook*, "à la carte" means "on the house." Free, a caddy's favorite phrase. Music to a caddy's ears.

Free.

Chew on that for a bit.

It's Masters Sunday, but not the one you're familiar with. This is the Sunday *before* the Monday start of the tournament. Three days of practice rounds with the Par 3 tournament thrown in for levity and TV ratings that will one day touch the moon, with the stars not far behind. This is Masters Sunday, the day an *Augusta* caddy, a local caddy who knows her fairways and greens like a mama knows her baby's every move, gets a bag for the tournament. A golden goose with a leather strap. Perhaps a ticket out of here—a Tour player on his way up. Or a seasoned vet, with only the motions to go through, a pro on his way down the ladder of perceived success, with dusty trophies and interest building bank to remind him of what could've been, what *should've* been, what wasn't meant to be.

The triumvirate of almost.

But if he's an older gentleman, with his playing days long in the rearview mirror, rest assured he's a Masters champion and they can't take that away. Freddie always said there ain't no luggage rack on a hearse, and there ain't no dress code for the Pearly Gates. No jacket required, but if you want to wear that green one, well that's just fine with the man upstairs.

55

Yes, it's a Masters Sunday for an Augusta National caddy, of which I am one, with two full seasons under my white jumpsuit. Thanks to Freddie, I have learned at the knee and gesturing finger tips of the best there is—Masters winners all. Bear, Skinny, Edward, Johnny Ball, Leon McCladdie, Jerry Beard, Hickey, the list goes on, and the greatest runner-up of them all, Mark Eubanks, Johnny Miller's three-time runner-up caddy and maybe not so proud owner of a sack full of top-tens. I've come to know Mark well. He gave me my caddy house nickname: White Boy. It may not be the most clever or insightful, but it fits me like a good pair of skivvies, something not every caddy wears, especially on the hot days.

As Freddie says, you don't read Augusta's greens, man. You *remember* them. I'd forget my own name before I'd forget the ghost break on number two with the ball below the hole. It breaks right, sometimes a lot, even with the cup leaning toward the clubhouse like a barfly at closing time.

On these greens, if you go just by what you see, you may as well tell your seeing eye dog to get back in the Cadillac courtesy car.

It's Masters Sunday, circa 1992. I only wish it were '72; then I would be surrounded by a sea of my caddy brethren, me standing out like a bobber with no fish on the line. But I got me one on the way.

All the way from Phoenix, Arizona.

"College kid," says Freddie. "Plays from the wrong side of the ball but can hit all the right shots, especially with that damn wedge. He can shave you so close with that thing you won't need the barber for a month of Sundays!"

One of which is today.

Freddie's right about the college kid playing from the wrong side of the ball. His clubs are, well, they're backward. Left-handed, like Hogan, before Hogan switched over to the right side. This kid plays from the Dark Side. Well, I'll bring him to the light, or I ain't Obi-Wan of the fairways.

I spin the kid's lob wedge, pull out my damp towel, and start wiping down the rest of his clubs, though there's no real reason to. These babies are shining like spinner bait.

This kid takes care of his stuff, no doubt about that. Keeps his powder dry, as my dad likes to say. That'll take you far in life, keeping your powder dry.

"Looks like he beat you to it," says Freddie, smiling as he rubs a finger on the backward blade of a 9-iron. "You can tell this kid's a player without even seeing him swing." Freddie holds up the modern-day niblick and points with his eyes a worn round spot on the clubface—the exact spot where a perfectly straight shot connects ball and clubface. I've only seen two this perfect before: Jack Nicklaus's sticks, and my step brother's, Andy.

"How'd he get here?" I ask.

"He sure as hell didn't walk," says Freddie, laughing. I laugh, too.

"No, I mean what'd he do to qualify for the Masters?"

"Oh, that," says Freddie. "Let's see. Won back-to-back NCAA titles at Arizona State, but that won't get you down Magnolia Lane. Won the Augusta College home tournament just last spring—your old stomping grounds—but that *damn* sure won't do it. Oh, yeah," Freddie snaps his fingers. "This long-hitting lefty won the US Amateur last summer. Threw a 64 on 'em at Meridian to lock down medalist and the number-one seed going into match play. Won pretty much every match in swashbuckler fashion, hitting par 5s in two and rolling in putts like a mop-haired Bobby Locke. This kid's long as a dateline and cocky as Lanny Watkins—and can back it up with a short game that'll make even Seve Ballesteros stop and take notice. And *that* som'bitch don't look at nothing but the mirror!"

I'm laughing hard when the door swings open, as is the kid who just bounced through it. An older fellow—though not by much—shuffles in behind him.

"Afternoon, gentlemen," says Freddie, coming from around his desk in a singular move. "How can I help you fellas?"

The response is quick, to the point, and it's painful as a kick in the biscuits.

"Uh, yeah. Hi, I'm Phil Mickelson. And, um, that's my bag, there." He points to the college bag balanced between my knees. I stop what I'm doing, but I don't get it. The tone of his voice stops me. It's like my ass is glued to the chair.

"I guess there's been some confusion," says the defending Amateur Champion. "My coach is gonna caddy for me. Sorry about that."

Your *coach*? I say to myself. Did he just say his coach, or his dad? Not that it makes a shit. He could have said Helen Reddy for all it matters now.

That bag is *gone*.

Freddie can see I'm crushed, but his face doesn't show it. Instead, he winks at me and slides the bag away. And just like that it really is gone, out the door and out of my life. So is the best, and as it turns out the *only* chance I ever get to caddy in the Masters.

"Well," says Freddie, sitting back in his chair, filling it with solid muscle and the smoke of a Marlboro Red. "He's still an amateur, so there wouldn't have been any prize money. For either one of you cats. But I know that ain't what you were looking for."

"No," I say. "That ain't what I was looking for."

"Hey," says Freddie, wiping dirt I can't see off his desk. "You hungry? Man, I am. How about some clam chowder? I'll get Chef to hook us up. Make you feel better, I'll bet."

I want to say you'd lose, but I don't. I just smile, but it's a fake one.

"It's just a bag, man," says Freddie, packing out another Marlboro Red. He lights it with a book of green matches, striking the lone match like you might flick lint off your shirt. The embossed, gold Augusta National Golf Club lettering glitters in the afterglow.

"Let's go bowl, not cup," says Freddie. "And I'll tell you all about the time *my* ass almost caddied in the Masters. But that hardheaded Frank Stranahan got us kicked off the course by none other than the man himself. Now ain't that some shit?"

"Mr. Roberts kicked y'all off the course?"

"It damn sure wasn't *Mrs.* Roberts."

"I've heard of Stranahan," I say. "He was going to be the next Bobby Jones."

"Shit," says Freddie. "He wasn't even Bobby Nichols."

"Whatever happened to him? Stranahan."

"Mr. Roberts is what happened to him. I got to come back. He didn't."

I smile. "Thank God for that," I say. "Augusta wouldn't be Augusta without you, Freddie."

"You right about that," says Freddie, spinning out his cigarette in the gold, logoed ashtray. "Let's go get us some chowder, man."

"Soup of the day?" I ask.

"It is now," says a smiling Freddie, patting me on the shoulder as we head out of his office and into April sunshine.

CHEF CLARK'S SECRET RECIPE
NEW ENGLAND CLAM CHOWDER

(SERVES 10-12)

Unless you're a clam, who doesn't love clam chowder? Nothing against the Manhattan version—I love that red brothy goodness and the city that birthed it, but there ain't nothing like a hearty bowl of New England Clam Chowder to warm the old bones and cockles of your heart. Q: Anyone out there know what cockles are? Bonus points if you do. A: Latin: *cochleae cordis*; from cochlea (snail) alluding to their shape, in this case the shape of the heart.

Augusta caddy master Freddie Bennett and longtime head chef James Clark shared a unique relationship. Think Butch Cassidy and the Sundance Kid. They made sense of the daily world around them in ways so few of us ever do.

Both lightning-witted and Edison bright, this just might be the cleverest recipe I ever came across during my halcyon Augusta days. You can learn an awful lot simply by observing, but I reckon you know that.

Now, let's go dig some clams!

I'm kidding. Thanks to the good folks at Bumblebee, we can leave the shovels in the shed next to those wading boots full of spiders. And while canned minced clams might not be as good on the surface of the tongue as fresh Little Necks from the Chesapeake Bay (on paper, they don't stand a chance), by the time we're finished whipping up this little dish, I challenge any purist to tell the difference.

Between you and me, ain't no way they can tell when you make it this well.

INGREDIENTS AND TOOLS OF THE TRADE

- 5–6 decent-sized red potatoes.
- Potato peeler.
- Can opener. Invest in a good one. A crappy can opener can make your kitchen life hell.
- Eight 10 3/4 -ounce cans of Campbell's Soup New England Clam Chowder.
- Good-sized pot, at least 7 quarts.
- 1 large black trash bag to hide the cans and other bits of evidence from roving eyes.
- School-milk-sized container (half-pint) of Land O'Lakes half-'n-half cream.
- 6 cans of Bumble Bee minced clams. Don't you dare drain the juice.
- Two 6-ounce bottles Bumble Bee clam juice.
- Your very sharp knife. The one that's now mentally hanging around your neck like a cross.
- Italian parsley, finely chopped. (fresh if you want to be a badass; dried if you just want to be an ass. I'm joking. Both versions work just fine, though fresh is prettier, like the way the dog Bucky from the comic strip *Get Fuzzy* feels when he wears his wristwatch. Fresh parsley also helps the chowder pass for homemade, which is the goal here, after all.)
- Favorite stirring spoon that will also double as a tasting spoon. It's OK—we're all family here.
- Wondra All Purpose Quick-Mixing Flour.
- Whisk—the kick-ass metal one.
- Chicken stock, like Kitchen Basics or Kirkland Organic.
- Insider's knowledge of the exact location of the light switch that turns off any lights illuminating the back entrance to your kitchen, so you can slip out the door with your black Hefty trash bag (courtesy of Freddie) full of incriminating (I prefer the word *discriminating*) evidence in tow. The trunk of Freddie's old Buick station wagon awaits!

PREPARATION

Let's get started.

I'd tell you to lock your kitchen door, but most homes don't have doors in their kitchens that do, and besides, what would the neighbors think?

My God, man. Just what on earth are you doing *in there?*

Wash the potatoes. Don't want any grit in the chowder. Unless you're an oyster, grit's a bad thing. Easy to remember. Grit is bad; grits is good. Take that, *21st Century Manual of Style*!

Leave the skin on the red potatoes. This makes your chowder look homemade. I only told you to get the peeler out in case someone happens by and asks: "So, what'cha makin' for dinner?"

In honor of Chef Clark, empty the cans of Campbell's Soup into the pot and turn the burner on low to medium—depending on how much time you have. The directions on the soup can will say add water or milk. Add neither. Substitute half-'n-half instead. Pour that goodness straight into the can, but not all the way to the top. Do this each time you open a can. If you want, you can add milk to one of the cans, but only one. Add in half the cans of Bumblebee minced clams and at least one bottle of clam juice. Finely chop the fresh parsley and dice up those unpeeled new potatoes, but be sure and dice them in irregular shapes, the essence of home cooking. If time is your friend, add the potatoes directly to the pot. If not, blanch separately and then add.

What do I mean by blanch? Well, I ain't talking about the office secretary in *Grease*.

Discreetly toss those soup cans into the bottom of the black garbage bag. As the chowder heats, add the rest of the minced clams. All of 'em. Don't drain, unless you really, really want to. This is canned pot liquor, baby. The au jus of the sea!

Add the chopped Italian parsley.

Take a moment to stir what you've got so far with that favorite spoon of yours. If things are a little too brothy, now's the time to add a little Wondra. Whisk away. If things aren't brothy enough, add a little chicken stock. Again, whisk away.

Let what you have cook a bit—coast, is the word I like to use. The chowder should thicken up a bit as it coasts, but not too much.

We ain't standing up spoons, here.

Once it's been 20–30 minutes, give the chowder a stir. Ease out a skin-on new potato and a clam or two, let 'em cool, then dive in for a sampling. Is anything missing, or is our work here done? It's fine to add an extra string of lights to the tree if you want. You've already made sure it's damn good. Now make sure it's your own. And as you do, share the story behind it all, black Hefty trash bags and well-loved Buicks included. Don't you *ever* forget where you came from.

Promise me that.

CHEF CLARK'S ROASTED LEG OF LAMB, WITH A SIDE OF JOB SECURITY

(SERVES 10-12)

INGREDIENTS AND TOOLS OF THE TRADE

- 1 GOOD-SIZED LEG OF LAMB—5–7 POUNDS, BONE IN OR OUT. THE BONE WILL CHANGE THE SHAPE OF THE LAMB AS IT COOKS, YES, BUT THE BONE'S DISCERNABLE EFFECT ON FLAVOR IS A MYTH.
- ALUMINUM FOIL.
- SHEET PAN.
- CEREAL BOWL FOR MIXING STUFF.
- 2 THUMB-SIZED SCOOPS OF DIJON MUSTARD.
- SEA SALT AND GROUND PEPPER.
- A FEW SPRIGS OF FRESH THYME.
- 1 GLASS OF WHITE WINE, PREFERABLY FROM A VINEYARD YOU LIKE.
- 4 GARLIC CLOVES.
- SARAN WRAP FOR COVERING (DAMN FLIES!).
- KITCHEN STRING.
- EXTRA VIRGIN OLIVE OIL, FIRST PRESS. KIDDING. REGULAR OLIVE OIL WILL DO JUST FINE.
- GOOD-SIZED ROASTING PAN, FOR COOKING THE LAMB AND TWEAKING THE AU JUS.
- A COUPLE SPRIGS OF FRESH ROSEMARY.
- MEAT THERMOMETER.
- GRAVY BOAT.
- SHARP-ASS KNIFE.
- SHERRY, THE KIND EPISCOPALIANS USE FOR COMMUNION. HIT YOUR KNEES AND PASS THE CHALICE, PLEASE!

PREPARATION

Unwrap the lamb and place it on your aluminum-foil-covered baking sheet. In that cereal bowl, mix the Dijon mustard, sea salt, and ground pepper, thyme, and wine. Crush up the garlic cloves and add them, too.

When you're happy with the mix, score the fat bit of the lamb with that sharp knife of yours and rub in the seasonings with washed fingers. Cover the lamb with Saran Wrap and pop it in the fridge for a couple hours, if time allows. Longer the better, but if time is *not* on your side, that's OK. Any marinade is a good marinade.

Tie the leg of lamb with kitchen string like you would a shoe, if a shoe were ever like a leg of lamb. When the lamb is ready (right now or two hours from now) bring it to room temperature and turn the oven to 425. (Not 451—we ain't burning books here.) Take a moment before putting the lamb in the oven and sprinkle the meat with salt, pepper, and olive oil. Hit all sides.

It ain't a home run unless you touch 'em all!

When you're ready to roll, put the lamb in the roasting pan fatty side up, and delicately drape on the rosemary, like you would a pashmina scarf on the neck of a beautiful woman. Do not cover. Cook for about 20–25 minutes. Unless you forgot to press start when you turned your oven on to 425 degrees, the lamb should brown up quickly, like ryegrass in July.

Now, ease the temperature down to 350. Think about 10–12 minutes cooking time per pound of meat for getting the desired doneness of medium rare. As much as I love to buck the system, here's where I write checks—and balances.

After about 30–40 minutes on 350 degrees, open the oven and check the lamb's temp by sliding a thermometer into the thickest part. A reading from the Book of Job. . . no, no, a reading of 130 is what you're hoping for. This, my friend, is the perfect temperature at which the lamb, once removed from the oven and allowed to rest like the Good Lord on the 7th Day, will become a beautiful medium rare, preferably more rare than medium.

Something to remember is when you put the lamb on the cutting board to rest, be sure and put it fatty side down this time. This will redistribute the juices.

Redistribute the juices. Now *there's* a phrase for ya!

Save those pan drippings for later. It's the au jus to end all au jus!

While the lamb rests (poor thing—he's had a long, hot day) you can do the next step one of two ways: You can pour all the pan drippings in a small pot, or simply leave them be.

Dash in a few splashes of sherry. Be sure and whisk the brothy goodness as you simmer the contents of the pot over a low heat. The au jus should thicken up a touch when it's ready. Pour the liquid magic into a gravy boat (if you've got one) and serve alongside the lamb, which may or may not be ready to slice into 1-inch-thick cuts with your new best friend, Mr. Sharpknife.

And that's it. Job secured. Hired for life.

A SOUTHERN CHEF IN PARIS

I f you know your way around the kitchen—and I mean *really* know your way around— you're probably familiar with Parisian potatoes. You may not be best friends, but chances are they've come to the family reunion once or twice over the years. Chef Clark's love affair with these crown jewels of the potato kingdom was born out of necessity—to impress his new boss Clifford Roberts and lock down his job as head chef of Augusta National Golf Club.

On the night Chef prepared his job-securing dinner for the founder of Augusta National, he pulled out all the stops, though he did leave a couple plugs in place for later, just in case (see Chef Clark's Secret Recipe Clam Chowder, page 59).

Privy to the knowledge that Mr. Roberts had peculiar, though for the most part healthy eating habits that leaned on the table of less done the better, Chef chose the safest vegetable he knew to complement his roasted lamb: the potato. He quickly surmised that the best way to showcase this well-known tuber was to dress her up in her Sunday best, and what better way to put a wig on a pig than Parisian potatoes? In a proper serving dish they look fancy as a ball gown, as complementary to any main course as a tuft of blonde hair curled along the chiseled cheek of Marilyn Monroe.

Mr. Roberts must have felt the same, having said after finishing his Chef Clark–prepared dinner of roasted leg of lamb with au jus drippings, Parisian potatoes, and port wine, beautifully concluded with his favorite dessert: pound cake, "Chef, I do believe this is the finest meal I've ever had the pleasure of being served at Augusta National."

And without further affirmation from the Club's founder, whose iron fist was often found wrapped in velvet, Chef Clark knew the job was his for life. And indeed it was, as James "Bollie" Clark held the position of head chef of Augusta National Golf Club for just shy of 30 years.

Rest in peace, Chef.

Augusta National ain't been the same without you.

CHEF CLARK'S PARISIAN POTATOES, WITH A NOD TO 21 CLUB

(SERVES 8-10)

INGREDIENTS AND TOOLS OF THE TRADE

- ABOUT 3 POUNDS OF YUKON GOLD POTATOES, WHICH IS AROUND 5–6 NICE-SIZED ONES. YOU CAN GO RUSSET, BUT ONLY IF YOU WANT TO BE DISAPPOINTED.
- POTATO PEELER.
- SHARP KNIFE FOR QUARTERING THE YUKONS.
- PARISIAN SCOOP OR MELON BALLER. OF COURSE YOU HAVE ONE. GOT IT FOR A WEDDING PRESENT AND THOUGHT, WHAT IN THE *HELL* IS THIS? WELL, NOW YOU KNOW.
- MEDIUM SIZED POT FOR BLANCHING THE POTATOES, ONCE PARISIANED.
- PROPER SKILLET FOR SAUTÉING.
- EXTRA VIRGIN OLIVE OIL. ALL THIS MEANS IS THE OLIVE OIL COMES FROM THE FIRST BATCH, OR PRESS. SO, DON'T BE. IMPRESSED, I MEAN.
- A FEW SPOONFULS OF PROPER BUTTER, LIKE KERRYGOLD OR OLIVIO.
- 4 GARLIC CLOVES. MINCED, UNLIKE MY WORDS.
- SEA SALT, AS OPPOSED TO THE SELDOM USED RIVER SALT, WHICH IS VIRTUALLY IMPOSSIBLE TO FIND THESE DAYS. ANY DAYS, FOR THAT MATTER.
- GROUND PEPPER.
- LARGE SPOON FOR STIRRING.
- FRESH PARSLEY. ITALIAN IS PRETTIEST.
- THAT GOOD-SIZED NONSTICK PAN I'VE BEEN HARPING ON YOU ABOUT GETTING.
- SERVING DISH. DEGREE OF FANCINESS IS UP TO YOU.

PREPARATION

Wash the potatoes.

Peel and quarter those Yukons. This will make it easier to scoop out the melon-shaped balls. Trying to scoop out a whole large potato can be a booger bear, let me tell you. Five to six Parisian potatoes per person is all you need, so multiply that times your number of guests (Finally! You get to use that middle school math in ways you only dreamed of), and you'll have a pretty good idea of how much work you have cut out for you.

After you get your scoop on, put the potatoes in a pot and cover them with cold water. (So, what do *you* do for a living? Who, me? Yes, you. Oh, I scoop out potatoes. Do you *really*?) I'm sure there's a scientific reason behind cold water versus hot, but damned if I know what it is. I reckon I slept through that day in class.

Bring the potatoes to a gentle boil and let roll for a bit until the potatoes are tender—they should whiten up a touch to let you know. If you don't know how to boil potatoes, I ain't telling you. But if you really want to be sure the potatoes are ready for the next step, gently stab one with a knife (Your honor, all I did was *gently* stab the victim) and if the knife slides out easily, the taters are ready.

Move on to that awesome skillet of yours and melt the tabs of butter over a medium heat. Drizzle in just a touch of olive oil. When you see a little sizzle, toss in the potato balls and minced garlic. Dash on a little sea salt and ground pepper, and gently roll the potatoes around in the skillet with that big spoon of yours until they're nicely covered with the goodness. Be sure to keep the burner on medium—you don't want to scorch.

Save that for when you iron your dress shirts drunk.

Keep this unique to the process, potato rolling ritual going for about 5 minutes or so, until the potato balls are slightly browned, like the color of aging copper. Sprinkle in fresh parsley (this is strictly for effect, aesthetics, and ambiance, as parsley has little to no flavor). Cook for another minute or two, swirling the skillet around like the pro you now are. Spoon those marble-shaped tubers out of the skillet and into that fancy serving dish. Serve hot. And just like the roasted lamb, that's it. Job secured. Well done.

Make that medium rare.

STANDING ON THE SHOULDERS OF GIANTS

I often talk of standing on the shoulders of giants. Those words are not original to me. Sir Isaac Newton beat me to it. But if you're going to get beaten to something, better a clever saying than a pulp.

Whenever I make Dream On, Maryland Crab Cakes, I find myself standing on the shoulders of three giants: Chef James Clark, Freddie Bennett, and my mother, Marion Cotton. I wish I knew where Chef got the recipe originally, but I'm afraid it's lost with him, and Freddie, too, as they smile down upon us. My mom's only memory of this simple yet so incredibly delicious recipe is Freddie sharing the secret at our home on Wheeler Road, back when I was a wee lad.

Calling them Dream On, Maryland Crab Cakes was my idea, though I suppose the joke's on me, seeing as how the essential ingredient is Old Bay Crab Cake Classic Mix, and, written on the package in small print that's not so small anymore, three words I've somehow missed for the past thirty or so years: *Original Maryland Recipe*.

But, you gotta give credit where credit is due—maybe *I'm* the one who should be dreaming on. In the meantime, I'll keep standing on the shoulders of giants. There's plenty of room up here, by the way.

DREAM ON, MARYLAND CRAB CAKES

(SERVES 3-4)

INGREDIENTS AND TOOLS OF THE TRADE

- One package of Old Bay Crab Cake Classic Mix. I typically don't use the whole package, hitting the brakes around 2/3rds gone.
- About 5 decent spoonfuls of Duke's mayonnaise, or any proper mayo—preferably one you would choose if you love mayonnaise and knew you only had one week to live. Life is too short for light mayonnaise. As the great comedian and satirist Lewis Grizzard once said about healthy eating: Do you *live* longer, or does it just *seem* longer?
- 1 shot glass of red onion, chopped as fine as that beau in seventh grade you had a crush on.
- 1 shot glass of fresh parsley.
- 1 shot glass of chives.
- Enough sprinkles of pepper to make you happy.
- Dash of table salt.
- Double dash of Old Bay Seasoning.
- Dusting of tabasco sauce or cayenne pepper. I actually like the cayenne pepper. Seems to spread the flavor out more evenly, though I have no idea as to why.
- Thimble-worth of dry mustard. This is a recipe must.
- Good-sized mixing bowl—always give yourself plenty of room to work—whenever, or whatever, you mix.

- A SPOON YOU LIKE, OR THAT REALLY COOL WHISK I'VE BEEN TALKING ABOUT.
- LEMON WEDGES FOR DRIZZLING.
- 1 POUND OF *LUMP* CRABMEAT. PHILLIPS PREMIUM CRAB LUMP WILD CAUGHT IS, IN MY MIND, THE ABSOLUTE BEST, IF YOU CAN GET IT. I'D LIKE TO MEET THE PERSON WHO PICKS THE MEAT OUT OF THE CRABS WHERE THIS SUCCULENT LUMP MEAT HIDES AND SHAKE THEIR NICKED-UP HAND, 'CAUSE THAT IS ONE *HELL* OF A JOB. YOU CAN GO WITH CLAW MEAT, WHICH I ALSO LOVE, BUT IT JUST WON'T BE THE SAME. CALL IT THE DIFFERENCE BETWEEN GOOD, AND GREAT.
- OLIVE OIL SPRAY, LIKE BERTOLLI.
- FAVORITE NONSTICK PAN, OR ELECTRIC SKILLET—IF YOU WANT TO ROLL OLD SCHOOL.

PREPARATION

With your whisk, swirl and mix everything together, except for the crabmeat and lemon wedges. If time allows, and I highly recommend this, let your crab cake mix chill for a little bit. (Overnight is ideal, but any chill time is better than no chill time.)

Add the lump crab meat to your chilled and seasoned mix a small handful at a time, using your fingers. Do what's called folding it in, even though that usually means giving up. In this case, it means you're giving in to the gods of great taste. You do not want to hide lump crab meat inside the cakes—you want to be able to see the prize your eyes are on, especially when you pay 26 bucks a pound for it!

When you're happy with the mix you can do one of two things: You can shape 'em medallion-sized like my mom does, which are quite tasty, and your crab cakes will go a *lot* further. Medallions are about the size of a 50-cent piece.

The other way is my way, and that's to shape the crab cakes about the size of my hamburgers—about 1/3 pound each. Talk about making an impression—and friends you never knew you had.

Once your crab cakes are patted out and formed to your liking, put your favorite nonstick skillet on the stove, turn the heat to medium, spray in a little olive oil (even though the pan is nonstick), give it a bit to get hot, then ease in the crab cakes one at a time, careful not to crowd or break.

They say the way to a man's heart is through his stomach. Maybe so, and maybe this will get you there. But it also doesn't hurt to be sweet and kind no matter whose stomach you're going through or whose heart you're after.

Cook your crab cakes a few minutes each side—you can tell by the sound of the sizzle when they're brown enough to flip—a skill I'm confident you've learned by now. So flip, lower the heat and let 'em sizzle a little more. A cool trick here is to take a clear pot lid (so you can see what the heck's going on) and put it over the crab cakes, trapping in heat and a bit of steam—a sure-fire way to cook crab cakes all the way through and ensure a warm, moist, dream-like edible experience.

Yes, it's just that good.

Turn off the stove and slide your skillet to another burner (preferably one that's not on), leaving the lid in place till you're ready to serve. But—if you want a little crunch with your crab cakes, take the lid off. Don't forget the lemon wedges.

And that is it, my friend. You just made the best crab cakes you'll ever eat! That wasn't so hard, now, was it? The credit card bill of 26 bucks a pound for crab meat—now, *that* might be a little hard to take.

OFF-THE-CHART CRAB CAKE TARTAR SAUCE

(ENOUGH FOR ONE POUND OF CRAB CAKES)

When your crab cakes are this good, I don't want to say you could take or leave tartar sauce, but you can take or leave tartar sauce. Unless, of course, it's *this* tartar sauce. I can't say I've had this born-in-France crab cake condiment anywhere but in the good ol' US of A, but I *can* say I've never had it quite this good. "Unforgettable" might be an unusual choice when it comes to describing tartar sauce, but that's the word that comes to mind.

INGREDIENTS AND TOOLS OF THE TRADE

- 3 DIME-SIZED HITS OF DILL RELISH.
- ½ A SHOT GLASS OF MINCED RED ONIONS.
- ½ A SHOT GLASS OF CHOPPED CAPERS (I KNOW—THEY'RE PRETTY DAMN SMALL TO BEGIN WITH).
- ¼ SHOT GLASS OF CHOPPED ITALIAN PARSLEY.
- COUPLE GOOD SQUEEZES OF FRESH LEMON JUICE.
- DASH OF TABASCO SAUCE.
- 6–8 SPOONFULS OF DUKE'S MAYONNAISE.
- MIXING BOWL.
- SPOON FOR TASTING.
- SPOON FOR SERVING. SMALL GLASS BOWL OR DISH, ALSO FOR SERVING.

PREPARATION

Grab your favorite mixing bowl and mix everything together, until it looks like creamy, white paint with bits of red onion and capers mixed in. Give it a taste. If it savors on the taste buds unlike any tartar sauce you've ever had before, you're home.

Spoon and serve this magic in a glass bowl or dish. This sauce is worthy of showing off, and the red onions, parsley, and capers give it a nice color. Be sure to slide a small serving spoon into the tartar sauce so folks can self-serve. You're busy enough as it is.

If you ever dreamed of serving the best crab cakes this side of the Free State, guess what? They just came true. Now go dream of something else, like a laundry genie who washes and folds without asking.

THE POT ROAST GRANDMAS ONLY DREAM OF

If Sundays are a day of rest, then God never caddied at Augusta National, where Sunday is often the busiest day of the week. Certainly, Sundays are one of the most crucial when it comes to business decisions—business decisions that can only take place on links the likes of Augusta.

That three-day bag that flew in on Friday in time for a quick 18 and maybe the par three, making up for any grass growing underfoot by squeezing in 45 holes on Saturday? Well, they're on the first plane westward soon as they putt out on 18. If you haven't worked out a tip by then, that tip wasn't meant to be worked.

Now comes the tricky part. The coin flip, the dice roll. Do you grab a quick bone sandwich and tell Freddie you'll gladly take whatever bag comes rolling through the parking lot, even if it's a trunk-slammer (a local member), also known in the caddy yard as Mr. Rule, with The Rule being the committee-approved fee for caddying at Augusta?

Back in my day, it was thirty-five bucks for the Big Course, twelve for the par 3—fifteen if you caddied all eleven holes. The original first two holes of the par three course were, in their heyday, absolute gems. From tee to green both were just a couple 60-yard butter-cut sand wedges, very indicative of George Cobb and John LaFoy's clever way of lulling you to sleep—good night, Irene—before ripping off the Band-Aid and all the hair attached on holes 3–9.

Sadly, those original holes are all but ignored these days, often spending their days flagless, with holes uncut and greens much slower on the stimp.

So do you roll the dice on the chance of a three-day bag flying in with the off chance they'll play 18 before dinner—there was as good a chance of that as the group not playing at all, and equally as good of not riding down Magnolia Lane until Monday morning, even Monday afternoon.

When your jet is as private as your life, it's a lot easier to come and go as you please.

Whoever said, "Time waits for no one," never waited in a caddy yard for an out of town bag. As for rolling the dice, in my caddy days I was more of a bird in the hand kind of guy. Those firethorn bushes can be awfully prickly, whether you make it to the back 9 or not.

Sundays at Augusta may not have been days of rest, but they were always days for pot roast—Southern style, with all the trimmings, even if sometimes those trimmings were just extra gravy (hold the potatoes because they weren't on sale and neither were the carrots). To my caddy brothers Tip Light and Donahue, this one's for you. May you rest in peace, or at the very least, get some rest.

I promise I'll go heavy on the gravy.

CADDY YARD POT ROAST

(FEEDS 8-10)

INGREDIENTS AND TOOLS OF THE TRADE

- 2 PACKS OF BONELESS CHUCK ROASTS, NICELY MARBLED. ABOUT 7 POUNDS TOTAL, BEFORE YOU TRIM AWAY EXCESS FAT.
- THAT REALLY SHARP KNIFE I HARP ABOUT.
- A CUTTING BOARD THAT WON'T WOBBLE.
- GOOD-SIZED POT. A LE CREUSET IS WORTH THE INVESTMENT 1,000 TIMES OVER, AND IF YOU DIE BROKE AT LEAST YOU'LL HAVE THAT TO LEAVE TO YOUR KIDS, OR THE DOG.
- COOKING SPRAY—YOU KNOW WHY I PREFER THE GRILL KIND.
- 2 PACKS OF LIPTON ONION SOUP.
- SOY SAUCE—GO LOW SODIUM, IF YOU CAN. THERE'S ALREADY ENOUGH SALT IN SOY TO CURE AN ELEPHANT. YOU DAMN SURE WON'T BE ABLE TO TELL 1,000 GRAMS ARE MISSING.
- WORCESTERSHIRE SAUCE.
- GROUND PEPPER.
- LEMON PEPPER.
- GARLIC SALT.
- CELERY SALT.
- ONE 32-OUNCE BOX OF KITCHEN BASICS CHICKEN STOCK.
- ONE 16-OUNCE CAN OF LIGHT BEER (OPTIONAL, BUT NOT REALLY).
- LEMON JUICE.
- 2 FAMILY-SIZED CANS OF CREAM OF MUSHROOM SOUP. GROCERY BRAND IS FINE

FOR THE WAY WE'RE GOING TO USE IT. THE WAY WE'RE GONNA DRESS HER UP AND TAKE HER DANCING, THE BRAND MATTERS NOT.

- ONE 10¾-OUNCE CAN OF CREAM OF CELERY SOUP.
- 2 PACKETS OF MUSHROOM GRAVY. BROWN GRAVY SUBSTITUTES JUST FINE.
- AROUND 16 OR SO OF THE SMALLEST NEW POTATOES YOU CAN FIND IN THE BIN AT THE GROCERY (OPTIONAL).
- ONE 16-OUNCE BAG OF CARROTS (OPTIONAL). GO BABY, TO SAVE A STEP. BUGS BUNNY STYLE IS FINE, TOO.
- GOOD SPOON FOR STIRRING AND TASTING ALONG THE WAY.
- FORK FOR TESTING TEXTURE.

PREPARATION

Remove the boneless chucks from the packages. Trim off any excess fat. It's fine if you find it easier to trim the roast by cutting the meat into large pieces. By large, I mean G.I. Joe action figure size, not the Lego World G.I. Joe. We ain't making stew meat, here.

Remember that skillet I didn't mention? Well, I still don't want you to use it. We're not going to brown the roast. I know that's often the rule of thumb, but you can probably tell by now we make our own rules here. Besides, thumbs are for hitchhiking, and I kinda like the ride we're on.

Spray your Le Creuset liberally with cooking spray and pop in the trimmed chuck roasts. Turn the oven to 375; this will *not* be the only temperature we use when cooking pot roast, but that's a good thing, Variety is, indeed, the spice of life.

Open a pack of onion soup and sprinkle over the roasts. Dash on all the seasonings: soy sauce, Worcestershire sauce, ground pepper, lemon pepper, garlic salt, celery salt—all the usual suspects. By now, I reckon you know how much is just enough.

Pour in 1/3 or so of the chicken stock and half a can of beer; squeeze in some lemon juice. Mix and stir.

Add the cream of mushroom and celery soup, spreading evenly. Dash on a bit more seasoning if you think it needs it, but be careful of overkill. Ghosts *will* appear and fade away.

Open the second pack of onion soup and mushroom gravy. Let 'em fall down like snow flurries onto the roast. Add a little more Worcestershire sauce and a touch of soy. A little ground pepper won't hurt. Close the lid.

The lid, Patrick. The lid.

Slide the pot into the oven, turn your kitchen timer to 1:45 and go do something else. I'm sure you have plenty on your plate.

When the timer dings, carefully open the oven and lid and see what you've got so far. Both the mushroom and celery soup should be blending in nicely, with just a hint of their former selves. Stir things up a little; push the roasts back down in the juice if you need to—chances are you will. If there's time and I hope there is, turn the oven down to 325. But, if you're as pressed for time as flower petals in Grandma's Bible, leave the temperature right where it is. Either way, set the timer for about 1:15. I know we're jumping around a bit on temperature and time, but this is how you learn how much is how much when it comes to time, temperature, and texture as it relates to the perfect pot roast. With a nod to the everwise Harvey Penick: Practice does not make perfect. *Perfect* practice makes perfect.

When the timer goes off for the second time, pull the roast from the oven, put it on an unlit burner, and remove the lid. Everything should look beautifully melded together, or at the very least headed in that direction. Take your fork and take a stab (at the roast, then at what you think the next step may be). When the roast is ready, the meat will pull away like the inside of a loaf of sourdough bread. If it doesn't, and most likely won't just yet, that's OK. Stir a little, put the lid back on, slide the roast in the oven, and turn the heat down to 275. Set your timer for 45 minutes.

Go do something else, but stay close.

When the timer dings, open the oven door, easing out the roast just enough to sample the goods. Carefully remove the lid to avoid a face full of steam. Test the roast with your trusty fork. If it's telling the truth, your roast should be as tender as filet mignon in most sections. If so, it's so close to perfect it could be a Bible verse. Put the lid back on and set the timer for 30 minutes. Your work—hope it wasn't work, but fun—is almost done.

After 30 minutes of coasting, pull the roast from the oven, remove the lid, step back, and admire your handiwork. That's a mighty beautiful roast you got there, my friend. As good as anybody can make.

This time, that anybody is *you*.

EXTRA HOLES: POTATOES AND CARROTS

If you're wanting to add a little something extra to an already amazing dish, pop in some small new potatoes—as is, no need to slice them—and also the baby carrots, with about an hour or so left on the clock. Using your hands, put 'em in the pot, *carefully* placing both potatoes and carrots where you think they should go around the finishing roasts. Spoon on the au jus gravy to cover both veggies and roasts before putting the lid back on.

If you go want to go Bugs and not baby, be sure and slice the carrots Tinkertoys style.

The reason I add the new potatoes and carrots so late in the game is twofold. Though new potatoes are far less likely to turn to mush than russet or gold, an hour of cooking time is plenty. Maybe it's just me, and no offense to Bugs's favorite food, but in my oven carrots cook quicker than the books at a parlay palace, and a little carrot flavor goes a long way, no matter what recipe road you're traveling.

When it's all done to your liking, serve at your leisure. This wonderful dish is as good piping hot as it is room temperature, unless, of course, you live in an igloo.

THE FIRST SIGN OF SPRING

I'm not sure what they look for in other parts of the country, but in the Deep South the first sign of spring is a robin. In Freddie's office at Augusta National Golf Club, however, it was something altogether different. Something about the size of an onion. In fact, that's exactly what it was.

A *Vidalia* onion.

Sitting in the catbird seat that was Freddie's black leather office chair, I was privy to many unique Augusta National experiences: Jack Nicklaus stopping by to chat with Freddie about the leather grip on his 1-iron; Arnie coming in to talk about life; Ben Hogan taking the time to sign his name beneath an incredibly life-like pen and ink drawing of himself and the aforementioned Jack and Arnie.

The no-autograph-signing Ben Hogan stopped by Freddie's office to sign his legendary name in the most legible handwriting imaginable. Stopping by only because Freddie asked him to, after Freddie pointed out to Ben that the other two golfers in the drawing were, in fact, looking *up* to him.

"As well they should," said Bantam Ben, in a voice only Freddie could hear.

But no experience at Augusta was quite as unforgettable as this: the official first rite of Spring, according to the belle of the farmyard ball. That belle, of course, was none other than the Vidalia onion.

Every year in early April, a gentleman named Jerry would knock on Freddie's door, wave hello, and enter with a croker sack of Vidalias thrown over his shoulder, like Santa Claus four months removed from his longest night of the year.

"First Vidalias of the season, Freddie. Won't be any more, either, unless you say so."

Freddie smiles and offers his chair, the one I'm sitting in. The two men shake hands.

"Hey, Mr. A. How've you been, sir?"

"Good, Freddie. Things are good. How about you?"

"Tolerable well, Mr. A. I can't complain. And if I did, there ain't no one around that would want to hear it."

The old man laughs and plops the sack of onions on Freddie's worn, wooden desk. I can't help but notice it's been recently polished, the smell of Glade, like office cologne.

"Well, what'cha got here?" asks Freddie, as if he doesn't already know.

Freddie leans over, opens the sack of onions, pulls out the biggest one he can find. With a trained hand, he eases off the papery skin before digging in with a fingernail to orange-peel a layer. He holds the onion up to the ceiling, turns it full circle, and before I can ask why, splits the onion into perfect halves.

Try doing *that* sometime.

The only sound in the room is the crack of a splitting onion, and a gasp if I could make one. With deft fingers, Freddie reaches into the Vidalia and pulls out the perfectly halved centerpiece, shaped, oddly enough, exactly like a teardrop. Freddie hands one half to Mr. A, the other half to me.

"You first, son," says Mr. A. "Tell me what you think."

It's a raw onion, I want to say. *Yuck*, I want to say. But because it involves Freddie, I pop the onion center into my mouth thinking: *I can get away with not chewing*. But the sugar cube sweetness cues my bicuspids and I can't help but use my teeth for what God intended.

My goodness, this is an onion? But it's sweeter than bubble gum!

I chew that onion until there's nothing left, swallow down the sweetness, and shake my head in utter disbelief.

"I'll take that as a yes," says Freddie, a smile on his face equaling my own.

Mr. A., playful as he slaps Freddie's desk, reaches over and grabs the old rotary phone. The Black Bat, Freddie's private line at Augusta. The number you called when it was important and the only person who could make it right was Freddie.

"I better tell the boys to get to harvestin'," says Mr. A., swallowing the last bite of the sweetest onion known to man.

"Miles to go before they sleep," says Freddie.

The Robert Frost reference is not lost on me.

CADDY YARD BREAKFAST HASH

(FEEDS 6-8)

─────────

I wish I could say something deep or otherworldly about this recipe, but I'd be making it up. *Well, my God! Man. That never stopped you before!*

This breakfast dish is an absolute delight, as easy to make as first grade math is to a fourth grader, and a saving grace like no other after a long night of caddy tomfoolery, or mornings when Freddie didn't serve up his lifesaving butter beans, and it was either take a knee or pray for pork chop sandwiches.

The only catch—not that I'm throwing anything—is you gotta first make that hall of fame pot roast, which, of course, you've already made. Congratulations. You can skip step one.

INGREDIENTS AND TOOLS OF THE TRADE

- WHAT'S LEFT OF THAT PHENOMENAL ROAST YOU JUST MADE FOR SUNDAY LUNCH (OR WAS IT DINNER). NOW YOU KNOW WHY I HAD YOU MAKE TWO!
- GOOD SPOON FOR STIRRING.
- TRUSTY ELECTRIC SKILLET OR GOOD-SIZED NONSTICK PAN. LIDS TO MATCH.
- 1 BOX KITCHEN BASICS OR KIRKLAND ORGANIC CHICKEN STOCK.
- 1 PACKET OF LIPTON ONION SOUP MIX. YOU MAY NOT NEED THIS, DEPENDING ON HOW MUCH GRAVY YOUR POT ROAST YIELDS.
- COUPLE SWEET ONIONS. VIDALIA, IF YOU CAN FIND THEM. IF NOT, JUST MAKE SURE THEY'RE SWEET.
- KITCHEN BOUQUET.
- GROUND PEPPER. ALWAYS, THE GROUND PEPPER.

- WONDRA FLOUR, YOUR NEW BEST FRIEND WHEN IT COMES TO MAKING GRAVY. BEGONE, LUMPS!
- SEASONINGS. BY THAT, I MEAN THE USUAL SUSPECTS.
- 4–5 PALM-SIZED WHITE OR YUKON GOLD POTATOES. DON'T CUT THE CORNER AND USE THE ONES YOU MADE EARLIER IN THE HALL OF FAME POT ROAST. THEY'VE ALREADY HAD THEIR DAY IN THE SUN. IT'S TIME TO SHINE ON A NEW DOG'S ASS.
- FAVORITE SQUISHY WHITE BREAD, OR SQUISHY WHOLE WHEAT BREAD.

PREPARATION

Shred the pot roast with a large fork or use your fingers. The roast pieces should be about flat-toothpick-wide and the chunks the size of the rocks you carried in your pockets as a kid.

With that spoon you've grown to love and know, scoop and scrape all the remaining gravy from inside your Le Creuset and put it in your skillet. If you cooked it right—and I know you did—even the gravy clinging to the edges of the roast pot will be worthy of salvage. It may be a darker shade of gold than the rest, but I promise it will be wonderful. Have a taste right now, if you like, channeling the days of sneaking a finger-pull of forbidden icing from your birthday cake long before the candles were lit and the presents unopened.

Now add the shredded pot roast to your electric or stovetop skillet and take stock of what you've got. Using your best judgment (with the burner or skillet knob on medium), add the chicken stock and Lipton onion soup, stirring here and there as you do. Add the chopped and diced onions, the usual suspect seasonings—again, using your best judgment and not an error in judgment—like the poor fellow in the excellent sleeper movie *Duets*. Stir. Add a dash of Kitchen Bouquet, ground pepper, and if you want to thicken things up, a flurry or two of Wondra. Stir some more.

Slice and cube the Yukon Gold potatoes. The size of a dice is ideal, but that can be trickier than sock-footed bowling, so just get close as you can to dice size and you'll be fine.

Add the cubed potatoes and stir.

With the lid off, keep a close eye on the goings on in your skillet for the next five to ten minutes. The breakfast hash should begin to gently bubble, like lumbering lava unsure of whether to flow into the nearest unsuspecting village or stay put.

Pack your bags, kids!

Stir. Wait for the bubbling to get good and even across the skillet horizon. When it does, put a lid on it. Let your breakfast hash roll like this for 20 minutes or so. It's fine to sneak a peek, especially as the aroma starts filling the house.

When you close in on 30 minutes, test those potatoes. They should be fairly tender and therefore ready, which means your breakfast hash is ready. But before you serve it up and wow the hungry guests staring fork holes in your back, break out a loaf of squishy white bread, adding a slice to every bowl or plate. I prefer a bowl. Makes it easiest to spoon out the last drop. Or, lick it out.

Both methods are equally acceptable.

Now, with the magic spoon of yours that's racking up love points left and right, serve up the breakfast hash on slices of squishy white bread.

Your breakfast hash.

I bet you nailed it.

Recipes are road maps to the soul.
—Lillie Winfield, circa 1984

PART II

THE INWARD 9

Junction/juhngk-sh*uh*n/
NOUN
1 the state of being joined; union
2 a place or point where two or more things meet
—Dictionary.com

THINGS AN AUGUSTA NATIONAL CADDY MIGHT CARRY IN HIS POCKETS

- 40-ounce bottle of malt liquor, discretely consumed in ye olde gravel parking lot prior to hiking the hills.
- Pine needles to freshen and/or disguise your breath.
- Fried pork chop sandwich.
- Bone sandwich.
- Sausage dog.
- Candy bar.
- Van-O Lunch crackers.
- Can of Beanee Weenee.
- Can of sardines.
- BBQ Corn Nuts. Also good for disguising beer breath, and, oddly filling, in spite of their small size.
- Kool Menthols in the box.
- Bic disposable lighter/book of Augusta National matches.
- Nip Chee sandwich crackers. All varieties.
- Boiled egg, shell on.
- Planters salted peanuts.
- Green yardage book, also known as The Green Bible.
- Handful of tees.
- Golf ball, preferably two. Exact brand and (hopefully) number of the ball your player is spraying all over God's green earth, so you can drop into a much more playable lie—at your discretion, of course.
- Wad of cash, from George to Benjamin and every president in between.

- Folded cup of grape soda.
- Folded cup of Coca-Cola.
- Wad of toilet paper—when you got to go, you got to go.
- ANGC pencils and scorecards for both the Big Course and Par Three.
- Silver coins for marking the ball.
- Sharpie for identifying your player's ball.
- Green bag of green dirt that is a pain in the ass to carry—for filling in divots, should your cold-topping player ever make one.
- Half-eaten roll of Tums—some days are longer than others.
- An extra smile, just in case yours turns upside down. *Never* forget how lucky you are to be caddying at Augusta National. I know I never did.

BONE SANDWICHES AND CADDY QUIPS

It's the first week in May and it's hotter than a snake's ass in a wagon rut. I'm schlepping my second 18 of the day with fellow Augusta caddies Tip Light, Donahue, and the ever-clever Mac, who calls everybody "Hey, baby," be they member, guest, or just one of the fellas.

Sweat is dripping down from every pore of the poor. I won't say downtrodden—we caddies, at least when we don the white jumpsuit and set foot on the fairways of Augusta, were as important to corporate America decision-making as the Dow Jones or any chairman of the board. A happy CEO is a very good thing, and few things bring happiness to the world's most influential decision-makers like a curling 20-footer holed out on the most fabled greens in golf.

Holed out thanks in part to the well-remembered reads of yours truly and his caddy brethren.

Yes, for at least four hours inside the guarded gates of Augusta National, we caddies were as important as anybody in the world sitting upright and taking nourishment. Especially right now, while walking up to the treacherous 14th green, which looks like a sloping Kilimanjaro with ghost breaks aplenty. And even though the sun is beating down like John Henry's sledge hammer, the oft watered fairways of Augusta are soft and damp. There's mud on the members ball—this simply will not do—and Mac aims to correct that little issue, only his towel is laying in the middle of 13 fairway where it slipped off his bag and landed on the grass soft as a butterfly with sore feet. The ever-resourceful Mac turns his attention to Tip Light, who's steady-studying his man's putt like it's an English exam written in Chinese. Tip rubs his temples with purpose, mumbling to himself in a language even he can't understand.

It's hard to tell if he's giving his man a read or crying for help.

Mac leans in to the mumbling Tip Light and says, "Hey, baby. Speak up where we can hear ya."

Tip stops rubbing his temples and squints, even though the sun is now behind a wall of wispy clouds. If Tip had glasses, he'd push them up the bridge of his nose.

"Say what, now?"

"Never mind, baby. Just let me hold your towel for a second. I gotta clean my man's ball. We about to make us a putt."

"What's wrong with *your* towel?" asks Tip, who's returned to rubbing his temples with authoritative fingers that tap as much as they rub.

"That's no concern of yours, baby. You just keep on rubbing holes in your head and hand me that towel. I'll give it right back. Mine's dry, and I know yours is wet."

"How you know my towel's wet?"

Good question, Tip. I'm wondering the same thing. The closest water fountain is to the right of 12 tee and 13 fairway, and since we've been moving slow as cream rising on buttermilk, that water fountain was 45 minutes ago. We've passed Rae's Creek twice, but I know Tip Light is scared to death of snakes. He wouldn't dip his towel in that creek water if Jesus Christ was walking on it!

Mac puts his big hand on Tip's even bigger shoulder.

"Tip, your towel wet from all them tears you been crying from all them bad reads you been giving your man. Now go on and give him another bad one, so that towel'll be good and wet when you hand it over."

Tip Light raises a finger at Mac and says, "Don't you start that shit with me." He turns to his man and says with words that are more question than statement, "Gimme two cups on the right, and don't deviate. Augusta National ain't *no place* for a devious man."

Mac laughs—a big ol' cackly guffaw, but it's good-natured.

"When's the last time you opened up a dictionary, baby? When you were looking up the definition for 'bad read'? Now, gimme that damn towel before you hurt yourself." Mac winks at me and pats Tip on the arm, thanking him for the wet towel as he wipes off the member's Titleist. "Cup and a half on the right, Mr. C., and don't deviate. This ain't no place for a devious man. Ain't that right, Tip?"

"As right as my reads," says Tip, his big mitt in the air as the returned towel hits its mark.

As right as my reads, I say to myself, laughing as I bite into the last of my bone sandwich. Dinner and a movie ain't got *nothing* on this.

THE SECRET TO CLUBHOUSE FRIED CHICKEN

(SERVES 4)

———————

Like most secrets, the secret to the absolute best fried chicken I've ever eaten isn't all that complicated. In fact, it's as simple as your ABCs, unless you're a two-year-old. In that case, it's complicated as hell.

Jokes aside, there is nothing smoke and mirrors about this tried and true fried chicken recipe, and there's nothing like a tin of Old Bay Seasoning for allowing the chef in you to not just *stand* on the shoulders of giants but to become one yourself.

INGREDIENTS AND TOOLS OF THE TRADE FOR SOME SERIOUS FRIED CHICKEN

- 3 CUPS FLOUR (BUT DON'T DEVIATE).
- SALT, BE IT TABLE OR SEA.
- GROUND PEPPER.
- 4 POUNDS CHICKEN; BASICALLY, A WHOLE CHICKEN YOU CAN CUT UP.
- DEEP PAN FOR DUSTING THE CHICKEN.
- OLD BAY SEASONING.
- CAKE RACK FOR DRYING THE SEASONED CHICKEN.
- PROPER OIL FOR FRYING.
- ELECTRIC FRYER—THEY SELL FARBERWARE AT WALMART. GET YOU ONE!

PREPARATION

Take the flour and mix with dashes of salt and pepper.

Put the chicken in a deep pan and season all sides with Old Bay Seasoning, rubbing the magic dust into the chicken with your clean fingers. Dust the chicken with the flour mix and spread out on a cake or wire rack to dry—about 10 minutes or so. Add oil to your electric fryer and crank the heat to 350—a light should illuminate to let you know when it's ready to roll.

Fry the chicken for 10–12 minutes. Like the Tripp's Chips (see page 117), you'll know the chicken is ready when it's floating in the oil. Remove with tongs and put the chicken on a paper-toweled plate and pat dry to remove any excess grease. Serve hot—or cold.

Despite the many changings of the proverbial guard at Augusta, this unique yet simple fried chicken recipe has quietly survived the test of time. Nice to know some things don't change.

A CADDY'S SECRET TO CHEF CLARK'S GREEN BEANS
(POLE BEANS, IF YOU GREW UP IN THE COUNTRY)
[SERVES 12-16]

No stranger to a canned good, Chef James Clark was as at home around a leg of lamb and Parisian potatoes as he was around Campbell's Soup and Sara Lee. And, according to lore that is replicated in many a country cooking restaurant to this day, canned green beans had a place in Chef's heart as well.

If you find yourself in dire need to whip up a pot of green beans for the ages and there's not a fresh pole bean climber to be found, try this simple little recipe and I guarantee the only person at the table that'll know the difference is you. And even *you* won't be able to tell—these green beans are just that good. The secret? They gotta be whole.

So watch and learn. Actually, make that *do* and learn. You're the one steering the ship, now.

Where to next, Captain?

INGREDIENTS AND TOOLS OF THE TRADE
- GOOD-SIZED POT FOR COOKING THE GREEN BEANS.
- TWO 32-OUNCE BOXES OF KITCHEN SECRETS CHICKEN STOCK, OR KIRKLAND ORGANIC.
- 1 HAM BONE. HONEYBAKED HAM BONES ARE THE BEST.
- WAX PAPER FOR COVERING THE HAM BONE.
- EIGHT 14-OUNCE CANS OF WHOLE GREEN BEANS. DEL MONTE IS AN EXCELLENT BRAND, BUT AS LONG AS THEY'RE WHOLE AND NOT CUT OR FRENCH, ANY BRAND WILL DO.
- LARGE BOWL FOR SOAKING THE GREEN BEANS.

- COUPLE PACKS OF CHICKEN GOYA SEASONING.
- ALL MY FAVORITE SEASONINGS: GARLIC SALT, CELERY SALT, LEMON PEPPER, LEMON JUICE, GROUND PEPPER, PEPPER VINEGAR—JUST A DASH AND SPLASH OF EACH.
- FORK FOR TESTING THE TENDER GOODNESS ON THE HAM BONE.
- TRUSTY PAIR OF TONGS.
- FAVORITE SPOON FOR STIRRING AND SAMPLING THE GOODS.

PREPARATION

Fill about ⅓ of your good-sized pot with water. Pour in a box of chicken stock and add the ham bone. Boil.

Drain all eight cans of whole green beans, using a colander so you don't lose any down the sink. If time allows (if for some reason it doesn't, you're wasting yours) fill a large bowl with cold water, add the drained green beans, and swish, rinse, and repeat four or five times. If you can't make time for this step, pour all the beans in the colander and rinse thoroughly, like you would pasta.

With the ham bone good and boiling, add the beans and seasonings, just like you did with the collards, clam chowder, and everything else we've rolled out so far. Remember—the only way to know is to know, and the only way to know is to do. There are *no* shortcuts for doing. That's why these recipes work, just like a repeatable golf swing.

Ben Hogan's, not Benihana's.

Turn down the heat a bit, so the boil is still boiling but not rolling. Let this go for half an hour, maybe. You can't cook green beans too long, far as I'm concerned. Don't worry that you might be cooking out the nutrients. Like unicorns, there's no real proof of that being true. But if you did manage to cook them out (the nutrients, not the unicorns), they're now in the pot liquor, which you'll soon be drinking, so all the better.

Speaking of, after a while taste the green bean au jus pot liquor. Need anything? A little more chicken stock, maybe? Sprinkle of celery salt, touch of ground pepper? Your phone, your call.

Test the ham bone with a fork or washed fingers. You're looking for the meat closest to the bone, just like with the collards. This, my friends, is the most succulent meat there is. If it feels like you could pull it off the bone like you might a dangling leaf off a tree, take out the ham bone with your trusty tongs, place it on a juice-catchable-plate, and cover with

wax paper. Let the ham bone cool. Stir the beans. If you notice them falling apart, even splitting, that is a very good thing.

When the ham bone is cool to the touch, remove what fat might still be on the meat and gently pull the ham nuggets away from the bone. By nuggets, I mean chunks. The meat closest to the bone—the best of the best, doesn't pull in slivers.

Admire your bounty. Stir the beans. Admire them, too. Breathe in the goodness. Taste. Does it need anything? Besides the ham, I mean. If it does, add it. If not, simply drop in the ham nuggets, shredding them slightly as you do. Hopefully, your ham bone yielded a plethora of close-to-the-bone goodness.

Stir, step back, and admire one more time.

And that, my friend, is a heaping pot of what should easily amount to the best green beans that you, and the folks you are kind enough to share them with, have ever had the good fortune and pleasure of eating. Remember, just because they're canned doesn't mean they're not good.

Or in this case, great.

FREDDIE BENNETT, PEACE MAKER

It's the Friday after Masters Week, and Augusta National is hopping like Black Friday at Walmart. Even though it's just my first full season at Augusta, it's clear to me that toting the rock inside these gates just might be the best job in the world.

My fellow caddy Curtis, however, might hold a different opinion, having spent the last 30 days under the care of the boys in blue at the 8th Street Jail. There are a number of reasons a caddy might find himself on the wrong side of boozeless bars, but this is a new one on me.

Child support. Not paying it, to be exact.

"That damn Curtis," says Freddie. "He's got babies all over town. You think by now he'd know what it takes to get 'em here. One momma found out about the other, and then all the mommas got together and turned his ass in. The wife, too. If you can believe that fool was ever actually married."

Freddie packs out a Marlboro Red but doesn't light it. "Man, he was so in arrears with unpaid child support he was inside out. Couldn't pay the ladies, so they made him pay the man!"

I'm picking up just pieces of what Freddie's saying, lost as I am in a saucer-sized crab cake to end all crab cakes. I've got pork chop sandwiches in each pocket, but as much as I love 'em, they can wait. Even cold, this crab cake sets records that will never be broken.

Freddie reaches under his chair, pulls out a four-pack of Long Life General Electric light bulbs and lays the box on his desk. He takes out a Sharpie, spins the bulbs around, writes a name on the side, and pushes it over. I recognize the name. In fact, we were just talking about him.

I stare at the box of light bulbs.

"She took everything, you know?"

"Who took everything?"

"Curtis's old lady. The last one standing. I know, I know—hard to believe the som'bitch was actually married. Justice of the peace, in an unjust world." Freddie laughs and lights his smoke with a green book of matches. "Of all the women Curtis procreated with, he finally made an honest woman out of one. But it takes a hell of a lot more than a wedding ring to unscorn a woman." Freddie shakes his head, spins the box of bulbs like a dreidel.

"Man, when I say she took everything, I mean everything. Washer, dryer, refrigerator, pillows off the king-sized bed that ain't there no more. The dust on the counter and the dust bunnies in the corner!" Freddie holds up the box of bulbs like he's examining a blood sample. He laughs, and it's contagious. I follow suit, even though I don't know what hand he's playing.

Freddie pushes the box of bulbs to the end of his desk and turns it so you can see Curtis's name, plain as a bagel on a plate of lox. It's the first thing you'll see when you come off the course and into Freddie's office to collect your day's wages, a decent mint if you were lucky enough to go 45 holes. I can't take my eyes off the box of bulbs, and even though I think I know the answer, I ask anyway.

"So, what's with the light bulbs, Freddie?"

Freddie laughs. "I told you Curtis's wife took everything out the house while his ass was in jail. I mean, she took everything but the paint off the walls. Even took all the damn light bulbs."

"Well, Curtis came home last night from the Big House to his house, flicked on the switch and the only light he saw was the Miller he was holding in his hand!"

I'm the one who's laughing now. Freddie's got more one-liners than Carter's got liver pills.

I'm taking my last bite of crab cake when Curtis walks in, fists in a ball and sweat pouring from his face. Curtis starts to yell something but thinks better of it. I get up with empty plate in hand and offer my chair. As bad a run of luck as he's had I figure he could use it. Curtis slumps into the chair, opens his fists, and buries his face in cracked hands. Without looking up, he mumbles, "Oh, goddamn, Freddie. What am I gonna do? That crazy woman took all my shit. I ain't got nothing but the shirt on my back. I ain't even got the toilet paper to wipe my ass!"

That's a damn good question, I think to myself. What *is* he going to do? Start over? But how? A caddy can only walk so many holes in a day.

Freddie pushes the box of light bulbs closer to Curtis, taps on the yellow cardboard package. Curtis looks up, sees his name.

"What's my name doin' on a box of goddamn light bulbs, Freddie?"

"You said your old lady took everything, even the light bulbs. Well, these might not get you back on your feet but at least you'll be able to see the som'bitches!"

Curtis looks up at Freddie and laughs till his empty stomach hurts, his darkened world suddenly a little brighter than when he first walked in. Freddie pulls six 20s from a thick stack of bills kept in a drawer, slides them under the box of bulbs. Curtis's wages for the day.

"Go down to the caddy house—get yourself something to eat," says Freddie. He taps on the crisp bills. "Keep these in your pocket. Tell Horace I said put it on my tab."

Curtis grabs the box of bulbs, folds the 20s and slides them into the front pocket of his caddy uniform, so everyone can see he just got paid.

"Thanks a lot, Freddie. I owe you one."

"You owe a lot more than one," says Freddie, winking at me so Curtis can see. He wraps a mailroom rubber band around the massive stack of bills, bends it like you would a deck of cards. The massive wad of cash goes back in the drawer.

He doesn't even bother to lock it.

CADDY YARD SAUSAGE DOGS

Like many of my favorite Augusta recipes, there's always that little something extra that makes them so special, and it never fails to surprise—even though I know it's coming. In the case of these sausage dogs, it's old-school yellow mustard for boiling.

Yellow mustard for boiling up sausage dogs?

I wish I could tell you otherwise, that I rubbed the dusty lamp of the snack genie and out popped some sort of magic seasoning that turned the typical sausage dog into one for the ages, but I can't. I've got the conscience of Abe Lincoln, and the bank account to prove it.

Crazy as it sounds, the next time you find yourself hankering for a sausage dog that will make you forget they make hot ones, squeeze a hearty helping of yellow mustard in the water before you boil, and see if I'm not right when I say, "Damn, that's a good sausage dog."

Mustard, eh? Who knew? Well, that would be me—and now, you.

INGREDIENTS AND TOOLS OF THE TRADE

- POT FOR BOILING THE SAUSAGE DOGS.
- YELLOW MUSTARD. I LIKE FRENCH'S, BUT I'LL BE DAMNED IF I CAN TELL THE DIFFERENCE FROM ONE YELLOW MUSTARD TO THE NEXT.
- 6-PACK OF SAUSAGE DOGS. GO WITH WHAT YOU LOVE—ITALIAN, BEER BRAT, HOT, MILD.
- TRICOLORED PEPPERS (OPTIONAL, BUT ONLY IF YOU THINK FLAVOR IS OPTIONAL).
- OLIVE OR VEGETABLE OIL FOR LIGHTLY FRYING THE SAUSAGE DOGS AND PEPPERS.
- GROUND PEPPER.

- GOOD PAN FOR FINISHING THE JOB.
- TRUSTY SET OF TONGS.
- TRUSTY, SHARP-ASS KNIFE.
- PACK OF BUNS. LIKE WITH THE KNIFE AND FORK CHILI DOGS, DON'T GO CHEAP HERE. A CRAPPY BUN WILL MAKE LIGHT OF ALL YOUR HARD WORK.
- TEXAS PETE HOT SAUCE.

PREPARATION

Fill your decent-sized pot half full of water. Squirt in enough mustard to make you say, "*Damn… That's a lot of mustard,*" when in fact it will hardly be enough to fill a shot glass. Drop in your sausage dogs of choice and boil, stirring occasionally, not because it will make a difference in the outcome, but because you're supposed to. Name a recipe that doesn't tell you to "stir."

If you've opted for the tricolored peppers, may I say excellent choice?

You may.

Slice the peppers lengthwise and drizzle on a little olive oil and a dash of ground pepper. Drop them in the heated pan and sauté, dancing them around until they're lightly charred and soft to the touch. But don't touch them. They're hot as hell.

With the tongs, pull the sausage dogs from the boiling yellow mustard and ease them into the pan with the peppers. Take that sharp knife and make some slices into the sausage dogs, about halfway in. This lets the juices flow—onto the peppers and into your heart.

Stir things up a little. This time it will actually make a difference.

With your trusty set of tongs, grab a sausage dog and slip it into a golden bun. Top it with a healthy pinch or two of the sautéed peppers. Squirt on a little more mustard for both flavor and aesthetics, the Texas Pete, too, if you dare. Now *this* is a good-looking sausage dog. Imagine how good it's gonna taste!

To that I say, stop imagining. Dig in, my friend.

THE BURGER PATTY AS GOD INTENDED, WITH A RESPECTFUL NOD TO THE GREATEST GOLFER THAT EVER LIVED

(SERVES 1)

If there's anything more American than the iconic burger, I do not know it. And if there's anyone who is more American to golf than Robert Tyre Jones, Jr., I do not know him. Or her.

Arnold Palmer might be golf to America, but Bobby Jones is American golf.

To that, I say try a burger as God intended. No condiments, no rising yeast. Just you, your favorite seasonings, and the freshest ground beef you can find.

INGREDIENTS AND TOOLS OF THE TRADE

- 1 POUND OR SO OF 73/27 GROUND BEEF, FRESH AS YOU CAN GET. BUY IT ON YOUR WAY BACK FROM THE COURSE AND COOK IT SOON AS YOU GET HOME.
- FAVORITE SEASONINGS—ERGO, ALL THE USUAL GRILLED-MEAT SUSPECTS SUCH AS GARLIC SALT, SOY AND WORCESTERSHIRE SAUCE, GROUND PEPPER, LEMON PEPPER, CELERY SALT.
- SPATULA FOR FLIPPING THE BURGER PATTIES.
- A GRILL YOU KNOW, LOVE, AND TRUST (NOTE THE ORDER IN WHICH THOSE WORDS ARE LISTED).
- RUBBERMAID TUPPERWARE OR LE CRUESET DUTCH OVEN FOR SEALING IN THE BURGER FLAVOR AFTER GRILLING.
- THE MAKINGS FOR A VERY DRY MARTINI. MIGHT I RECOMMEND BEEFEATER GIN, MARTINI ROSSI DRY VERMOUTH, AND A BIG, BEAUTIFUL, SEEDLESS OLIVE?
- THE MAKINGS FOR A *SECOND* VERY DRY MARTINI.
- YOUR FAVORITE POTATO CHIPS.

- PLATE FOR SERVING, PREFERABLY WITH UPWARD EDGES TO CATCH THE AU JUS.
- KNIFE AND FORK; NOT THAT YOU'RE GOING TO NEED THE KNIFE.
- NO BUN.
- NO CONDIMENTS.
- KNOWING WHEN A BURGER IS MEDIUM RARE AND HAVING THE WHEREWITHAL TO TAKE IT OFF THE GRILL A FEW MINUTES PRIOR TO. LIKE THE WAFFLE HOUSE ON CHRISTMAS DAY, IT KEEPS ON COOKING.

PREPARATION

Separate the ground beef into fairly equal halves to form a couple nice-sized patties, about the size of a flattened orange and half an inch thick. Season the burgers with the usual suspects.

Fire up your Weber.

Grill those burgers like I know you know how, taking special care to note when the center begins to bubble and ooze au jus. The moment they do, pull the burgers off the grill and place them in a bowl with a lid that seals—it's time for a little steam bath. I like to use my Rubbermaid Tupperware or Le Creuset Dutch oven (whichever is handy). Let the burgers coast for a bit while you make two very dry martinis.

Open the bag of your favorite potato chips and put some on your plate. Plain chips go best, but this is your burger, not mine. BBQ, sour cream and onion, heck—even dill pickle-flavored chips can suit just fine. Just be sure and leave ample room for that big, beautiful burger and savory cup of au jus.

Take a burger from the lidded pot or container and ease it onto your plate along with the cup of au jus. Take a well-earned sip of that lovely dry martini as you drizzle the warm au jus on your burger. Take a proper bite. WOW is the first word that comes to my mind, though you might think of a better one.

Now *that* is a burger as God intended, just as Bobby Jones played the game of golf as it was meant to be. Fun.

Golf was meant to be fun.

TRIPP'S CHIPS— HOME FRIES, CADDY YARD STYLE

(FEEDS 10-12)

———

Before I share the recipe for Tripp's Chips (which, by the way, are always a hit among old people, children, and puppies), first, a little back story.

Augusta National founder Clifford Roberts wasn't exactly what you'd call a health nut (not even sure such a moniker was around back then), owner that he was of the biggest sweet tooth this side of Willy Wonka, though I'm also not sure the ol' chocolatier ever actually *ate* any of his confectionary creations.

Either way, Roberts wasn't a big fan nor an advocate of grease, and if a member or guest ever walked into the Men's Grill (these days known simply as the Grill Room) looking for french fries, they'd better look somewhere else. Augusta's kitchen might have enough potatoes to feed the 5,000, but not a single spud ever blinked an eye at a vat of hot oil as long as Mr. Roberts was alive.

That's where the caddy comes in to save the day, the weeks, and even the months that follow. Why, a burger without fries is like Bogie without Bacall. Sailing away to Key Largo, my ass. We'll be lucky to raft down Rae's Creek!

A piping-hot plate of Tripp's Chips doused with malt vinegar and Bojangles seasoning, however, can make up for any number of sins.

INGREDIENTS AND TOOLS OF THE TRADE

- 6 PALM-SIZED POTATOES. YUKON GOLD OR WHITE ARE MY FAVORITE.
- SHARP KNIFE. MAY AS WELL HANG IT 'ROUND YOUR NECK LIKE A CROSS AS OFTEN AS I ASK YOU TO USE IT!
- FAVORITE CUTTING BOARD.

- BOWL FOR IMMERSING THE TRIPP'S CHIPS AS YOU WASH THEM.
- APRON—A REAL ONE (THIS COULD GET MESSY, BUT IT'S A GOOD MESSY, AND OIL IS A BITCH TO GET OUT OF CLOTHES, ESPECIALLY PINK COTTON GOLF SHIRTS.).
- FRYDADDY, GRANDPAPPY, OR ELECTRIC FRYER. YOU CAN GO WITH A DEEP SKILLET, BUT IT'S A LITTLE TRICKY TO TIME THE HEAT, OIL BUBBLES, AND RANDOM SPLATTER BURNS.
- OIL FOR SAID FRYER(S). VEGETABLE WORKS, BUT DROP THE EXTRA BUCKS AND GO PEANUT. GOOBER OIL HAS A HIGHER VISCOSITY, FOR YOU CHEMISTRY MAJORS. EVEN BETTER, IF YOU CAN FIND IT, IS SOYBEAN OIL. NOW *THIS* IS FRENCH FRY MAGIC! ALSO ON THAT ETHEREAL LEVEL IS THE SOYBEAN/PEANUT OIL BLEND.
- STRAINER SPOON.
- PAPER TOWELS.
- LARGE PLATE OR TRAY LINED WITH SAID PAPER TOWELS.
- MALT VINEGAR.
- SEA SALT AND GROUND PEPPER.
- POTATO PEELER (OPTIONAL).
- POTATO SCRUBBER (SEE: SPONGE).
- SEASONINGS. YOU CAN ROLL WITH THE OLD BAY STANDBY, OR SWING WITH MY MONKEYS AND GO BOJANGLES. BOJANGLES FRENCH FRY SEASONING IS SO GOOD IT SHOULD BE ILLEGAL IN MOST STATES. THEY SELL IT IN THE DRIVE-THRU, TOO.

PREPARATION

Grab a potato and give it a rinse.

Place the spud on the cutting board longways, holding the tater between your middle finger and thumb. Using great care and a knife sharp enough to filet a blade of grass and split a match all at the same time, slice that potato into thin circles, about the thickness of a silver dollar. If you're too young to know what that is, stack a couple quarters in your mind's eye and go with that. Or the thickness of a SweeTart.

When you're slicing tubers, be sure you know where your blade is at all times. Cutting, whether it's veggies, meat, or the hamstring of Judge Smails, is all about feel, just like putting. Freddie always said: If you can't putt, you can't play. Chef Clark may not have said it, but I bet he thought it: If you can't cut, you can't cook. Simple as that.

But I know you can cut. It'll take practice, a few flesh wounds, and a drop or two of blood on the cutlery, but if you learn how to cut the right way—no corners, all feel (the only way to learn feel is by doing), then you'll do just fine.

Now that you're bleeding like a stuck pig and your faith in mankind is shaken, take the remaining potatoes and slice them as thin as your confidence will allow. As close as you can to that silver dollar, stack of quarters, or SweeTart.

Once all sliced (sounds like the name of a really bad but undeniably readable true crime novel), drop the potato slices into a large bowl of cold water and keep rinsing until the water is clear as a cloudless sky. The water will at first be a bit milky, like the potatoes have been wearing sunscreen, but nothing a few cold-water baths won't cure. Drain the taters, pat them dry with a paper towel, add the oil to your electric fryer and plug it in. If you don't have an electric fryer, go buy one. I'll wait.

After about 10 minutes of heating the oil, drop in a test chip. You'll know it's ready when the chip sinks, then rises to the top in a kamikaze roll of bubbles. Remove so as not to burn the test chip. Add more chips. *Carefully.* Until you get the hang of it, dropping potato slices into a vat of very hot oil is a bit dangerous, akin to cliff diving.

I've never actually counted how many chips I put in the fryer at any given time, but if I were counting like Rain Man and this were Vegas, I'd say 18–20.

Let the frying begin.

We all know the cooking instruction *stir occasionally*. I personally have no idea what that means. Stir when the mood strikes? Before I pop the top on my third O'Doul's? What matters is what it means to *you*.

As you figure that out, stir occasionally, letting 7–10 minutes pass by. Depending on your fryer, oil of choice, and definition of stir occasionally, your Tripp's Chips should be nearing the home stretch. But unlike the Kentucky Derby, we don't want any Secretariats here. We want Robin Hood and his band of Merry Men. All for one and one for all. If you've sliced them the best you could with that SweeTart shape or silver dollar in mind, my money is on all the chips being done at the same time.

So, how do you know when they're done?

When the chips are floating in the oil like bobbers on Ike's Pond with a childhood summer breeze blowing and they're the color of your cane pole, your chips are done. With that spoon strainer that is now a welcome part of your kitchen tools arsenal, carefully scoop the chips out of the very hot oil, letting them drip-drain before shaking them onto the paper-toweled plate. Try not to stack the chips on top of one another if you can help it.

Spread 'em out like a game of solitaire.

With a fresh paper towel, do a little flippity-flop with the chips to soak up any extra grease, like you would bacon, if bacon were sliced, round, and fried in soybean oil. Scatter the Tripp's Chips on the serving plate. Try one, if you like. This is pre-seasoning. But unlike most preseasons, this one matters. If you've nailed it, the chips should be crisp and firm, with just a hint of flavor even though you've yet to salt and pepper, yet to malt and vinegar. Enough of a hint to make you smile and say to yourself and the dog at your feet: Hey, this is pretty damn good!

If you can do that, break out the sea salt and ground pepper, malt vinegar, and Bojangles Seasoning and season to your heart's content. You've earned the right, my friend.

And you thought your money was no good here.

THE SECRET TO A GREAT STEAK, AUGUSTA CLUBHOUSE STYLE

(SERVES 4)

Chef Clark believed that what makes for a great burger (see page 113) makes for a great steak. Like a strike-three from Koufax, Ryan, or Maddox, it's all in the delivery.

In golf, it all starts with the setup.

If you've played these sports with any degree of success, you know damn well that the art of hitting a golf ball or a baseball is pretty much the same. Different canvas, different brush, but the fundamentals of hitting the ball solidly are eerily similar, the swings virtually the same.

INGREDIENTS AND TOOLS OF THE TRADE FOR STEAKS WORTHY OF THE MEMORY BOOK

- FOUR 1 1/2-INCH-THICK RIBEYES. YOU CAN ALSO GO WITH FILETS OR PORTERHOUSE, IN HONOR OF THE CLASSIC *CADDYSHACK* LOCKER ROOM ATTENDANT. *WAX BUILDUP, HELL!*
- PAN FOR SEASONING THE STEAKS (AND A PAN FOR COLLECTING THE STEAKS FROM THE GRILL. CAN BE ONE AND THE SAME). FOR FAVORITE SEASONINGS, SEE PAGE 113.
- GROUND PEPPER.
- SEA SALT, PROVIDED IT'S GRANULATED.
- ONE HELL OF A GRILL OR OVEN. OF COURSE, AS KING OF AUGUSTA'S KITCHEN, CHEF CLARK HAD ACCESS TO BOTH.
- TONGS (OR WASHED HANDS—WHICHEVER YOU PREFER).

- FRESH ITALIAN PARSLEY (OPTIONAL).
- PROPER BUTTER, SUCH AS KERRYGOLD OR OLIVIO, SHOULD YOU WANT TO ADD A LITTLE TOUCH OF RUTH'S CHRIS.

PREPARATION

OK, let's grill.

Take the steaks from the fridge; unwrap and put them on a pan with a decent ridge around the edges. If time allows, let the steaks coast to room temperature, unless you've locked yourself in the walk-in cooler.

Season the steaks on both sides with sea salt and ground pepper. Keep the lid on the olive oil and the wrapper on the butter. Rub in the salt and pepper. Gently, like you would your knees if you were faking an injury. Fire up the grill. Follow the same steps as when we were making the Burger Patty as God Intended. She'll let you know when she's ready.

She's ready.

With your favorite set of tongs or washed hands à la chef Clark, place the steaks on the grill, an inch or so apart, letting them sizzle a good 3 to 5 minutes before flipping. You can strive for perfect grill marks if you like, but to me that's like striving for bruises to prove you played one hell of a game. Grill marks are pretty, but so are freshly cut flowers at a funeral. A nice, little uniform char on the steaks? Now that's a different story altogether.

After about five minutes of liking what you see, smell, and hear, flip the steaks. Now's the time, just like it was with the burgers, to learn what varying degrees of doneness *feels* like. The more the meat bends, flexes, or does the Triple Lindy off the high dive, the *rarer* it is. The less the meat bends, flexes, or does the praying mantis as it prances through summer zoysia, the *doner* it is. (Hey, is that like done and doner?)

It's up to you to learn the difference. I promise you will, if you haven't already.

Once the steaks are closing in on your desired doneness, pull them off the grill. I say "closing in" because although those beauties are no longer in contact with direct heat, they're still cooking—like a sunburn with the sun long set.

Place the steaks in the pan, the one you seasoned them in and subsequently washed. Cover lightly with *real* aluminum foil, like Reynolds Wrap. If someone asked for their steak

à la Ruth's Chris, add a dab of melted butter to their plate and sprinkle with Italian parsley. Keep it separate from the others. Wait a few minutes.

Call your guests to the table. But before you serve them the perfect steak, tilt the grill pan at an angle, so you can call up some of that beautiful ribeye au jus. Drizzle it on their steaks like fairy dust.

I always knew Tinker Bell was the smart one.

A RECIPE IN PERPETUITY

Take nothing from Hogan, Jack, or Tiger (notice I didn't say Bobby—you could *never* take anything away from him), but no one did for the modern era of golf what Arnold Daniel Palmer did, changes that are still in full bloom every time the Tour tees it up. Televised coverage of any and all events, purses so lucrative they could support third world countries, typical course conditions that rival (but not surpass) Augusta National. The list goes on and on.

But for everything we know about Arnie, who knew he loved chicken and dumplings as much as an up and down from the spinach? Chicken and *flat* dumplings, not the thick, biscuit-y kind most of us grew up on. I reckon all those years of putting the undulating, mountainous greens at Augusta would make any man go flat, even the King.

I'm privy to this curious bit of Arnie trivia not from the times he hosted the Masters Club Dinner, where the evening's eats are determined by the defending Masters Champion, nor from any book authored or coauthored, approved or disapproved, but from the proprietor of Calvert's Restaurant, the crown jewel of fine dining in Augusta, Georgia, for more than 40 years.

Tucked like a pocket square in the cashmere coat that is the Shops at Surrey, Calvert's is just a modern-day Par-5 from the gates of Augusta National. When Arnie was still blessing us with his larger-than-life, friend-to-all presence, Calvert's was Arnie's Masters Week home away from home, the King often stopping by after the Masters Club Dinner for cocktails and shared stories, shaking hands and posing for pictures with friends old and new.

Though Arnie loved pretty much everything on Calvert's eclectic, fine dining menu (think Lobster Savannah and grilled lemon chicken piccata), the King felt strongly something was missing, and wasn't shy about letting his proprietor friend know. That "something" was chicken and dumplings, Pennsylvania style, heavy on the Amish dumplings and chunks of dark meat chicken. After all, dark was more affordable than white, and more affordable was always a good thing for the Latrobe Country Club's superintendent's family that raised, nurtured, loved, and let fly the most charismatic, endearing, all-around genuine golfer the game has ever known.

"If you put chicken and dumplings on the menu," Arnie once told restaurant proprietor and Michigan-born converted southerner Craig Calvert, "they will come."

The proprietor smiled and stifled a laugh. He looked around at his packed house of a restaurant on that glorious Masters Week Tuesday, with the King of golf hardly an hour removed from his 25th Masters Club Dinner in a row, and said, "Where in the hell would we *put* them?"

CHICKEN AND DUMPLINGS, À LA ARNIE

(SERVES 10-12)

———————

To make this good ol' warm-the-bones recipe, you must first realize it also does a fine job of warming your heart, too. This is feel-good food, folks, just like Arnie was, and always will be, a feel-good player. What else could the greatest ambassador the game has ever known be?

If you put it on the menu, they will come.

What do you say, Craig?

INGREDIENTS AND TOOLS OF THE TRADE

- BIG-OL' POT.
- 2 PACKS OF BONELESS, SKINLESS THIGHS.
- THE USUAL SUSPECTS OF SEASONINGS: GARLIC SALT, LEMON PEPPER, GROUND PEPPER, CELERY SALT, PAPRIKA (FOR DUSTING THE CHICKEN THIGHS BEFORE BAKING), GOYA CHICKEN SEASONING.
- KITCHEN BASICS CHICKEN STOCK.
- GRUET BLANC DE NOIRS, FAVORITE CHARDONNAY, AND/OR BEER (OPTIONAL).
- SOY SAUCE.
- WORCESTERSHIRE SAUCE.
- WONDRA, FOR THICKENING THE STOCK, IF DESIRED.
- ANNIE'S OLD-FASHIONED FLAT DUMPLINGS.
- TONGS.
- JUICE-COLLECTING PAN.
- WAX PAPER FOR BRIEFLY COVERING THE BAKED CHICKEN THIGHS.

127

- LADLE FOR SERVING.
- BOWLS IN WHICH TO SERVE THIS WONDERFUL DISH.
- STRAWS FOR DRINKING THE STOCK. KIDDING—BUT IT'S GOOD ENOUGH TO AT
  LEAST MAKE YOU THINK ABOUT IT.

PREPARATION

Turn on your oven to 375.

Season the chicken thighs with the usual suspects, including paprika, soy, and Worcestershire. Continue by placing the chicken in your Dutch oven skin side up, so the flavor drips down. Add a little liquid: beer, wine, champagne, and/or chicken stock, enough so the thighs are wading in it. Drizzle on soy and Worcestershire sauce. Slide the pot into the oven. Now, turn your attention to the pot on the stove. Time to make a little chicken and dumplings pot liquor.

Pour in both boxes of Kitchen Basics chicken stock (or Kirkland Organic) into the stove pot, and turn the stove on medium.

STOCK. Commit that word to memory. With the exception of Goya, stock kicks bouillon's ass.

Work a little magic, here. Add in your seasonings, a little at a time—except the paprika. You can put that back in the cabinet. Add some water and a pack or two of chicken Goya. Taste what you got. If you like what's going down, get the pot liquor boiling and add the Amish dumplings one at a time, stirring as you go.

Yes, I know these dumplings are flat, and maybe not what you're used to. But I imagine this entire cookbook ain't what you're used to, yet it's been a heck of a lot of fun and you've been putting on a culinary clinic since recipe one! I'm proud of you. You should be proud of you, too.

Let the dumplings boil for 10 minutes or so, until tender, whatever that means to you. Tenderhearted? Tender footed?

Legal tender?

When the dumplings are *your* definition of tender, turn down the burner and turn your attention to the chicken thighs baking in the oven. Remove the pot and with tongs put the yard bird on a decent-sized, juice-collecting pan.

This is some *good* juice.

Cover with wax paper and let cool. When the chicken is cool enough to touch, shred the meat into bite-size slivers. Much like you would for barbecue, but a little thicker and less like blades of grass—more like ball marks on a green. Add these to what should now be a delectable batch of pot liquor and dumplings.

Stir and admire.

Add the drippings from the pan. Stir. Take a close look into the Dutch oven where you baked the chicken thighs. There will be some grease hanging around, but there's pot liquor, too. This is magic juice, as you well know. Spoon up as much as you can and add it to the dumplings pot. Stir and taste. If you like what's going down, close the lid and let things coast for 10 minutes. Lift the lid, stir once more, and admire your handiwork. I would.

If you put it on the menu, they will come. Long live the King.

CADDY YARD TUNA FISH SANDWICHES

(FEEDS 8-10)

In spite of the avalanche of fried pork chops, chicken, and sausage dogs that came out of Augusta's caddy house kitchen, it was a rare day in the caddy yard when I didn't show up with some sort of random food product of my own. Boiled eggs topped the list (they travel surprisingly well). Cool Hand Luke once ate 43 of these babies in one sitting, but I played hell to eat three.

I'm not going to roll out a boiled egg recipe on these pages. There are few tricks to the trade when it comes to boiling eggs, and in fact the only advice I can give is don't buy any cheap-ass eggs.

Now that we got *that* out the way, let's turn our taste buds to my favorite use of the ol' boiled egg: tuna fish salad. I don't care where you've had the best before. The Hamptons in the fall, early summer in the mountains of Rabun Gap, or even Mother's Day at the home of Kindly Mother Fletcher (no relation to my better half), I can promise you this: you've never had a tuna fish sandwich as good as the one you're about to make. If this tuna were NASCAR, it would be Richard Petty, BC Powders and all.

South's best tuna fish sandwich, anyone?

INGREDIENTS AND TOOLS OF THE TRADE

- 1 DOZEN LARGE OR EXTRA-LARGE EGGS. GO EGGLAND'S BEST AND STEER CLEAR OF THE HOUSE BRAND.
- FOUR 6-OUNCE CANS OF CHUNK LIGHT TUNA IN WATER, SUCH AS CHICKEN OF THE SEA. AFTER ALL, WHAT'S THE BEST TUNA? IN MY KITCHEN, WHITE TUNA IS OVERRATED. IT'S SIMPLY NOT GOOD FOR WHAT WE WANT TO DO HERE, AND THAT'S

131

MAKE SOME KICK-ASS TUNA FISH SALAD. SAME GOES FOR ALBACORE. TAKE THE WRONG TURN AT ALBUQUERQUE, BUT DON'T BUY ALBACORE TUNA. YOU MAY AS WELL BE EATING DUST.

- GOOD-SIZE MIXING BOWL.
- COLANDER FOR DRAINING.
- TWO 6-OUNCE CANS OF CHUNK LIGHT TUNA IN VEGETABLE OIL, BUT DON'T YOU DARE DRAIN.
- REAL DUKE'S MAYONNAISE. PLEASE DON'T GO LIGHT UNLESS YOU HAVE AN EXISTING HEART CONDITION. IF THAT'S THE CASE, WELL, NO ROLLER COASTERS FOR YOU!
- SLEEVE OF NABISCO SALTINES. SEA SALT IS OK, BUT DO *NOT* GET THE LIGHTLY SALTED. WHAT'S THE POINT?
- THAT SHARP KNIFE I KEEP TALKING ABOUT.
- CUTTING BOARD THAT DOESN'T WEEBLE, WOBBLE, *OR* FALL DOWN.
- 1 JAR OF CLAUSSEN KOSHER DILL PICKLES, SANDWICH SLICES. ALWAYS CHILLED, NEVER HEATED. I DON'T KNOW WHY THE CHILLED BIT MAKES SUCH A DIFFERENCE, BUT IT DOES. NOW THAT I THINK ABOUT IT, WHEN THE FLOOD OF '93 RIPPED THE GUTS OUT OF 11 AND 12 GREENS AT AUGUSTA, THE REPLACEMENT GRASS WAS TRUCKED DOWN FROM PENNSYLVANIA IN REFRIGERATED CARGO CABINS, SO MAYBE THE FOLKS AT CLAUSSEN ARE INDEED ON TO SOMETHING.
- PICKLE JUICE AND ALL THAT RANDOM LAVA LAMP-LOOKING STUFF THAT FLOATS ALONG THE BOTTOM OF THE JAR. FIND A WAY TO GET SOME OF THAT GOODNESS OUT. WE'RE GOING TO NEED AT LEAST A SPOONFUL OR TWO.
- VINEGAR, AND LOTS OF IT. DON'T BE SHY. PULL OUT THE STANDARD WHITE, RED, AND BALSAMIC. GO WHITE BALSAMIC IF YOU'RE WORRIED ABOUT CHANGING THE COLOR OF YOUR TUNA FISH, BUT UNLESS YOUR ITALIAN ROOTS ARE BAOBAB TREE-DEEP, YOU WON'T BE ABLE TO TASTE THE DIFFERENCE.
- FOR DUSTING PURPOSES: CELERY SALT, GARLIC SALT, LEMON PEPPER, GROUND PEPPER.
- GOOD-SIZE SPOON FOR MIXING AND STIRRING.
- SOFT AND SQUISHY BREAD. I DON'T REALLY CARE WHAT KIND, SO LONG AS IT'S SOFT. AND SQUISHY.
- TWO WEEKS' SALARY. I'M KIDDING. YOU COULD FEED THE WHOLE FAMILY FOR

UNDER 20 BUCKS WITH THIS DISH *AND* BLOW THEIR MIND WITH HOW GOOD IT IS. TWENTY BUCKS WELL SPENT, IF YOU ASKED ME. OR AS WE USED TO SAY IN THE CADDY YARD, "THAT DUB WILL HUNT!" [AUTHOR'S NOTE: A DUB IS A TWENTY-DOLLAR BILL, AS IN DOUBLE TWO TENS, AND A MCGARRETT IS A FIFTY-DOLLAR BILL, AS IN HAWAII FIVE-O. A CAT-EYE, SHOULD YOU BE SO LUCKY, IS A HUNDRED. HERE, KITTY KITTY.]

PREPARATION

Boil those eggs. While they're firming up, open the four cans of chunk light tuna in water, drain, and drop in a mixing bowl. Do the same with the two cans of tuna in vegetable oil but this time don't drain. This liquid is the juice, my friend. *This* we want to keep.

Squeeze in some Duke's Mayo—just a little, at first. Take the sleeve of crackers and pull out a handful. Crush 'em up over the mixing bowl.

Cut up some pickles, long ways then sideways, so the pieces are about the size of swollen Tic-Tacs. This is where sandwich slices come in handy. Saves a couple steps, and because they've been sliced already and spent their entire jarred life soaking up pickle juice, their flavor is off the charts. Ever wonder where flavor goes, once it goes off the charts?

A question for a wiser man than me, I suppose.

Add splashes of the vinegars you've got lined up like a wine tasting. By splash, I mean a capful of each. You can skip the cap and shake the vinegars out by hand, but you better be steady as a redwood.

By now the eggs should be boiled. Put them in the colander and roll cold water over their collective Humpty Dumpty selves for a few minutes. Resist the urge to pick one up. They may not look it, but chances are they're still hotter than Marilyn Monroe!

Once cooled, peel the eggs. They should peel easily, if you listened and bought good eggs and not Veruca Salt specials.

With washed hands, crumble seven or eight peeled eggs over the bowl of tuna, saltines, vinegar, and mayo. Dust in the celery salt, garlic salt, lemon pepper, ground pepper. Stir, and see what you've got. You want the consistency of meatloaf, crazy as that may sound. Blended chunky is a good way to describe it. If it's not, add what you think is needed. More crackers? (My mama taught me this to make the tuna go further.) More eggs? (A dear friend named Anne, quite the southern cook in her own right, taught me this trick during my Augusta caddy days to give the tuna fish salad color, texture, and a boost of unexpected flavor.) More pickles? (Anne again, for all the same reasons.)

More what? The answer could very well be: nothing at all.

Now, take that spoon, taste, and see what you got. If you don't go *wow*, keep going until you do. If you do go *wow*, reach for the squishy bread and make yourself a caddy yard tuna fish sandwich. Bless the bread with Duke's Mayonnaise, paper thin or nickel thick. Shake on a little balsamic for extra zing. Sneak a bite before you slide your sammidge into a quart-sized Ziploc. If you ever fall for the marketing ploy that is sandwich bags, I'm disowning you, like Neil Diamond's dad in *The Jazz Singer*. A sandwich bag will not even remotely hold a sandwich, at least not one that's a size worth eating.

Speaking of eating, if you finish your best of the South tuna sandwich before you so much as pull your black Trans Am into that ol' gravel parking lot reserved for caddies, grounds crew, and English majors, I won't hold it against you.

But the next time you make one, promise you'll make one for me.

THE VODKA FRONT ROLLS IN

In a world of food icons, from rhyming Ronald McDonald to first-name's-last Ruth's Chris, there is only one Jimmy Dean. Born a Leo on the cusp of the Great Depression, it's no small wonder Jimmy rose to the top, seeing as how the ol' crooner was smoother than a Velvet Elvis and knew every haggard line on Abe Lincoln's copper penny face.

Jimmy also knew his way around a hog's guanciale, though he first made his mark on the wall of success in country music, with the baritone ballad *Big Bad John*, a Grammy-winning ditty that crossed over into rock 'n' roll, where it also became a hit and later paved the way for *The Jimmy Dean Show*, a short-lived TV series that gave puppeteer Jim Henson his first national media exposure.

I first meet Jimmy Dean on a crisp, March morning, the sun shining down like a flare and the dew leaving reminders on the grass. Augusta's grounds are bustling with worker bees dressed in black pants and white shirts. Some sport waiter garb, some kitchen. Sous chefs and cleanup crews. Grounds crew folks on golf carts with shin-high Timberlands boots and shades, sun-stamped tans and expressions of purpose.

And then there's Jimmy Dean.

He's sitting forward in a convertible E-Z-GO golf cart, arm draped across the black steering wheel with no inclination to go left or right, forward or back. It's difficult to tell which arm is draped because he's wearing a long sleeve shirt. The morning air is crisp as lettuce, but not for much longer. Jimmy adjusts his hat as we pull up beside him in Freddie's personal golf cart—also an E-Z-GO but with the governor removed.

135

This baby will flat out fly!

I soon learn that in Jimmy Dean's world an adjusted cowboy hat means acknowledgment, but for Freddie, it's a term of endearment.

Jimmy locks eyes with Augusta's caddy master, grins like a possum. "Mornin', fellas."

Freddie smiles like the welcoming committee he is, genuine and heartfelt. If a smile could shake hands, Freddie's would.

"Good morning, Mr. Dean."

"Ah, damnit, Freddie. How many times I gotta tell you? I ain't no Mr. Dean. I'm Jimmy, just like you're Freddie. And today I ain't too much liking the weatherman. That boy can couldn't predict the winner of last year's Masters."

I look away from the rising sun and into a blue sky. It's a humid blue, the color of a faded Crayola. I'm no meteorologist, but it looks like a pretty nice day to me.

Jimmy Dean rubs his temple with his free hand, leaving the other one draped over the black steering wheel of the green E-Z-GO.

"It stormed something awful last night, Freddie. Lemme tell you. Vodka front blew in outta nowhere and didn't let up until way past midnight. Got so bad, I slept in my clothes with the lights on, fearing the worst." Jimmy shakes his head like a dog sprayed with a garden hose. His dark pants are ankle-length, covering most of the intricate design of his pointy-toed Ropers. He looks dressed for spurs and latigo, not lob wedges and one-putts.

"Thank God the storm dissipated, leaving this Texas boy none the worse for the wear."

I ponder this observation for a moment. Jimmy may be *saying* he feels like shit, but he sure doesn't *look* it. He looks dapper as Roy Rogers and twice as innocent. He winks at me—either that, or the sunshine caught him just right.

"So, no golf for me, Freddie. At least not this morning. I best rest up a bit, in case that vodka front rolls back around. Those storms'll do that sometimes, you know?" Jimmy Dean smiles and it's a grand one for the ages. He reaches over, shakes Freddie's hand. There's a crackling noise, and it ain't from a candy bar wrapper. Freddie's eyes brighten—as if they weren't diamonds already.

"I'll come check on you in a bit, Mr. Dean. Just to make sure you ain't checked out on *us*." Freddie laughs and works the wheel of the E-Z-GO.

"Jimmy, Freddie. Call me Jimmy. And don't you worry 'bout me—or anything else, for that matter. I didn't forget about you. Come see me this afternoon. I'll be around." Jimmy Dean adjusts his hat and nods in my direction. "Son."

Freddie promises we will, and we zip across the grass expanse and around the circle that fronts the clubhouse. We ease down the hill and park in front of Freddie's office. He holds the door for me and I walk inside.

I can't help but wonder what Jimmy Dean means by, "Don't worry. I didn't forget about you," seeing as he's already slipped Freddie a cat-eye. Turns out, I don't have to wonder very long.

After a quick 18 with a trunk slammer, caddy speak for a local member who is only here to play 18 holes and then hop in his Cadillac and head back home, I ease open the screen door to Freddie's office and flop down in a leather chair. The arms of the chair are worn from use, but the bones of my butt barely make an indention in the seat. Freddie doesn't look up, just opens his desk drawer and pulls out a familiar stack of bills, thick as a cowboy ribeye, and slides out three of them the way a magician might pull the ace of spades from a shuffled deck of cards. I don't bother putting the Jackson (20), Hamilton (10), and Lincoln (5) in order before sliding them into my wallet. They already are.

"Got a minute?" asks Freddie, knowing good and well I got minutes to spare. My main man Mr. B. won't be in for another three hours or more. I've got time on my hands, and empty pockets to put 'em in.

"Good," says Freddie. "Let's go."

I follow Freddie out the door and once again into his personal golf cart, the key in the ignition, the switch on. In all my years of knowing Freddie, I've seen it no other way.

It's a quick trip, this going back the way we came, and lo and behold there he is—Jimmy Dean, sitting in his convertible golf cart decked out to the exact same stylish duds as before, frozen in time like Marcel Marceau.

"There's my man," says Jimmy, pointing a finger at Freddie. "I told you I ain't forget about you." Jimmy pats the side of the large brown box on the seat beside him. Smoke-like vapors rise from the corners in tiny wisps you can almost see through.

"First sausage patties of the summer, Freddie. Just waitin' on you to fry 'em up. I know you know your way around a skillet, and I ain't about to insult your biscuit-making instincts."

Freddie laughs, and I can tell it's an old joke between them. Jimmy hands over the box of sausage patties, holding it with two hands, like a ring bearer.

"And I got something for *you*," says Freddie, pulling a glass jug from beneath his feet. He hands me the jug and I hand it to Jimmy. It looks like white lightning—moonshine—which is exactly what it is.

I'll let you guess how I know that.

Jimmy Dean just smiles, the cat that ate the canary. "And I thought that ol' weatherman said the storm was over," he says, holding the jug of 'shine by the handle, laughing as the afternoon sunlight bounces off the glass.

"Weatherman's been wrong before," says Freddie, returning the smile and laughter. He covers the box of Jimmy Dean Summer Sausage with a brand-new Masters towel as we slowly drive away.

No rush, this time.

CADDY YARD
SUMMER SAUSAGE AND BISCUITS

(SERVES 12-16)

INGREDIENTS AND TOOLS OF THE TRADE

- 3 CANS PILLSBURY DOUGHBOY BISCUITS—*I LOVE* SWEET HAWAIIAN-FLAVORED.
- COOKING SPRAY.
- CUTTING BOARD SMOOTH AS A ROSE PETAL—OR 2 METAL COOKIE SHEETS, GREASED.
- 3 OR 4 TUBES JIMMY DEAN SAUSAGE. MILD, HOT, MAPLE, SAGE—I LIKE 'EM ALL.
- SHARP KNIFE.
- SEASONING—ALL THE USUAL SUSPECTS, LIKE GROUND PEPPER, CELERY SALT, GARLIC SALT, SOY, AND WORCESTERSHIRE. SAUSAGE IS JUST GROUND BEEF SPELLED DIFFERENTLY.
- PROPER BUTTER LIKE KERRYGOLD OR LAND O'LAKES FOR MELTING IN THE SAUSAGE PAN.
- FAVORITE IRON SKILLET OR NONSTICK PAN.
- GLASS LID THAT'S JUST A LITTLE TOO SMALL TO FIT FLUSH WITH THE PAN.
- TONGS FOR FLIPPING THE SAUSAGE PATTIES.
- 2-PLY PAPER TOWELS.
- PAPER-TOWELED PLATE.
- GALLON ZIPLOC FOR STEAMING THE FINISHED SAUSAGE BISCUITS.
- YOUR IMAGINATION. I KNOW IT'S EARLY IN THE MORNING, BUT I BET YOU STILL GOT ONE.
- REYNOLDS WRAP ALUMINUM FOIL.

PREPARATION

Before you peel back the blue and orange wrapper on the container of biscuits, rub the Dough Boy's belly for luck. He's a biscuit Buddha, and your new best friend.

Crack open the biscuits, whopping the can on the counter angry grandma style. As the dough springs to life, turn the oven to 375. Notice I didn't say "preheat." Whoever came up with that instruction never cooked hungry. There's no need for preheating here.

That's what oven lights are for.

Shape the biscuits by simply pulling them apart—that Dough Boy has done the hard work for us. Spray a cookie sheet and place the biscuits on the sheet, about a golf ball-length apart. Pop them in the oven and set the timer to 10 minutes, knowing you will likely go 15. Biscuits aren't like bad haircuts. Once they're burned, there ain't *no* going back.

Turn your attention to the tubes of Jimmy Dean sausage.

With your very sharp knife, carefully slice the sausage into circles about the thickness of a Tinkertoy wheel (sound familiar?), or your pinky finger. Put the slices on a greased cookie sheet, press down and mold with your fingers. Irregular shapes are encouraged.

Season the patties with sprinklings of the usual suspects, like Worcestershire, soy, garlic salt, lemon, and ground pepper. Fire up the stove—medium heat is the road I like to take. Drop a dollop or two of proper butter in the pan, letting it melt before adding the sausage patties. Wait for the sizzle. Shouldn't take long. After about 3–4 minutes, flip the patties for the first time.

Check the biscuits. Yes, that means opening the oven door. They should be about halfway ready (has it been 7 minutes?), beginning to turn the color of a sunrise.

Now for the sausage magic trick: turn the heat down just a touch and place a glass lid over the patties, trapping in the steam, flavor, and sizzle, creating a mini sausage Atlantis! After a few minutes, lift the lid. Using tongs, gently press down on the biggest patty. It should bounce back like a military bedsheet. If it does, remove the patties and place on a paper-toweled plate. Dab off the grease—but not the flavor—with a two-ply paper towel. If you scrimped here on the paper towels, you'll know it.

Open the oven door and slide out the biscuits. They should have about 12–15 minutes on the kitchen clock (note: cooking times may vary my ass—they *will* vary, so it's important to keep an eye on them). Let the biscuits cool, but not too much. As soon as you can safely touch them, open those biscuits and slide in a sausage patty one at a time—unless you can do two at a time, but that would be a first. Put the finished sausage biscuits in a gallon

Ziploc bag and let them steam. After five minutes, remove the sausage biscuits and serve. Talk about good.

As Jimmy Dean liked to say: "In the mornings, you need something to kinda warm up the whole body, to get it going."

I say, "That'll do, Pig."

Author's note: Augusta National caddy and surprisingly agile tennis player, Don "Tip Light" Johnson, would wrap his sausage biscuits in aluminum foil and hawk them for a dollar apiece. They looked more like quarters in Tip's big hands. The biscuits were often as hard as a sprinkler head, but the sausage always hit the spot, even when that spot was moving.

Rest in peace, Tip Light. Your work here is done, old friend.

THE HALFWAY HOUSE AT AUGUSTA NATIONAL

FEATURING THE EVER-POPULAR MELVIN

In the Deep South, we have a rather definitive restaurant called the Varsity, known far and wide as the World's Largest Drive-In. According to legend (and Google), the Varsity sells enough hot dogs per day that if you were to place them end to end they would stretch to the moon and back. That's a lot of hot dogs! And a lot of stretching the truth.

The Varsity also has one of the best welcome greetings ever, hollered the moment you walk up to the counter by a server rocking the old-school red and white paper Varsity hat. Carhop hats, 60 years removed.

What'll ya have!?

The halfway house at Augusta has a similar greeting, minus the friendliness. It's unspoken, but the message is loud and clear: "You ain't getting nothing, caddy, until I take care of the member and the guests. Now move your ass on out the way."

"But I just want—"

"I just told you what you want, caddy. *Nothing!* And nothing is what you gonna get, till the players get theirs first."

"That's OK, Melvin. Like the fox from *Aesop's Fables*, I didn't want them grapes anyway."

Ol' Mad Dog Melvin.

Sweet Jesus! was he angry at the world.

Hired by someone who had no idea what it was like to caddy on an empty stomach in humid Augusta heat while wearing a jumpsuit that doubled as body wrap with your throat dry as an uncle's favorite joke, Melvin was the keeper of the halfway house flame. In this case, that meant drawers stuffed with Nip Chee crackers, Nekot cookies, and Bar None candy bars. In full view are blood-red apples and bananas yellow as the flag flapping on the ninth green, but unless you're a spider monkey with a getaway car, I suggest you look elsewhere for sustenance. Crackers? Yes, you can eventually have some of those. Fruit? No way in hell. Not unless you catch some falling from a pine tree. Wait. That would be pine nuts.

Nope, can't have those either. Transfusion? Maybe. All depends on Melvin's mood.

Well, what do you know? Looks like he's in a good one. I think he even smiled, or maybe that was just the morning sunlight bouncing off angry-at-the-world cheeks as he handed me a straight-up transfusion.

Say, Melvin. Any chance for a refill?

CAN I GET A WITNESS?
OR AT LEAST A TRANSFUSION?

(SERVES 8)

INGREDIENTS AND TOOLS OF THE TRADE FOR RECEIVING LIFE-SAVING, AUGUSTA NATIONAL CADDY PLASMA

- 1 PINNED-TO-YOUR-HAT CADDY BADGE WITH YOUR NAME ON IT, WRITTEN IN BLACK SHARPIE, BY YOUR OWN HAND.
- ONE 64-OUNCE BOTTLE(S) OF WELCH'S 100% GRAPE JUICE.
- A PLETHORA OF 12-OUNCE CANS OF SCHWEPPES GINGER ALE.
- STACKS OF 12-OUNCE GREEN WAX PAPER CUPS FOR SERVING. VIRTUALLY IMPOSSIBLE TO FIND ANYWHERE BUT AUGUSTA NATIONAL GOLF CLUB.
- LOTS OF ICE.
- SILVER MIXING SPOON WITH A REALLY LONG HANDLE. FOR MELVIN, THIS WAS MORE FOR SHOW THAN SUBSTANCE. WHEN YOU POUR GINGER ALE INTO GRAPE JUICE, IT MIXES ON ITS OWN JUST FINE. BUT MELVIN SURE LOVED TO PUT ON A SHOW WITH THAT DAMN SPOON, ESPECIALLY ON REALLY HOT DAYS WHEN HE KNEW YOU WERE CAMEL-THIRSTY.

PREPARATION

For those making transfusions at home, simply take equal parts Welch's Grape Juice and Schweppes Ginger Ale and pour into a large cup of ice, then another, mixing as you go, since you are kind enough to forego the really long spoon. Make the next pour into the cup you'll be drinking from, and voilà! You've just made an authentic, Augusta National transfusion.

As for making an authentic, Augusta National *con*fusion, follow the steps above and add a shot of Purity Vodka.

Make it a double, if you just doubled 18.

FOR THE LOVE OF FROGMORE STEW

(FEEDS 14-18)

=====

Freddie Bennett grew up in the Carolina Low Country, population not that many. Home to hard living and even harder times, the Low Country was also home to some of the best-tasting shrimp you ever washed down your gullet.

You know the old adage, "Must be something in the water"? Well, this was no adage; this was the God's honest truth, as written in stone as the 10 Commandments, with a gray-bearded Moses eager to part the intercoastal waterways of the Atlantic, seine nets in tow.

In honor of the Low Country waters Freddie seined for shrimp, gigged for flounder, and the woolly land he hunted for wild boar, I bring you one caddy's take on Low Country Boil, or, to speak in the language of origins, Frogmore Stew. In older circles it's called Tidewater Boil, which is a beautiful summation of this life and the people we come across, both as we enter this world and as we leave, riding the almighty wave until it crashes one last time.

Cowabunga, friends.

INGREDIENTS AND TOOLS OF THE TRADE FOR ONE OF MY ALL-TIME FAVORITE DISHES

- BIG-OL' POT.
- ACCESS TO RUNNING WATER, BE IT TAP, CREEK, OR INLET.
- BEERS, FOR YOU AND THE BOIL.
- OLD BAY SEASONING. THERE SIMPLY IS NO OTHER THAT COMPARES.
- WHITE VINEGAR. THERE ARE 1,000S OF *THESE* OTHERS.
- KNIFE, SHARP AS AN EMINEM RAP. ("I'M NOT AFRAID," AND NEITHER ARE YOU.)

- CUTTING BOARD.
- KIELBASA, AND LOTS OF IT. HILLSHIRE IS MY GO-TO. SMOKED, BEEF, OR POLSKA. EITHER OR ALL THREE WILL WORK JUST FINE.
- ABOUT 4 POUNDS OF CAT-PAW-SIZED NEW POTATOES, SKIN ON. DON'T PEEL 'EM UNLESS YOU WANT MUSH ON YOUR PLATE AND MUD IN YOUR EYE.
- A COUPLE RED ONIONS, AS MUCH FOR AESTHETICS AS FOR FLAVOR. IMAGINE A CHRISTMAS TREE WITHOUT TWINKLING LIGHTS. THAT'S LOW COUNTRY BOIL WITHOUT RED ONIONS.
- SWEET ONIONS, WHICH AREN'T THE SAME AS WHITE ONIONS. WHITE ONIONS ARE ABOUT AS SWEET AS VERUCA SALT. NO EVER-LASTING GOBSTOPPER FOR YOU, YOU LITTLE SHIT! GO VIDALIA IF YOU CAN, THOUGH I KNOW THE SEASONS DICTATE.
- LEMONS OUT THE WAZOO. BAG O' LEMONS IS BEST. DON'T GO JUMBO, UNLESS YOU HAVE A HANKERING FOR LEMON ZEST. WHICH, OF COURSE, HAS ABSOLUTELY NOTHING TO DO WITH THIS RECIPE.
- AT LEAST A DOZEN EARS OF CORN, SHUCKED, AND SNAPPED IN HALF IF YOU'RE FEEDING LITTLE ONES. THERE AIN'T NOTHING LIKE SUMMERTIME CORN. SILVER QUEEN (SOUNDS MORE LIKE A DRAG QUEEN THAN A VEGETABLE) IS KING, BUT THE WAY WE'RE ABOUT TO COOK IT, ANY CORN IS GOOD CORN.

PREPARATION

Fill that big ol' pot about 1/2 full of water and beer. Drizzle in Old Bay Seasoning and shake in some white vinegar, about a shot glass worth. With your sharp knife and handy cutting board, slice the kielbasa thumb length, the other side of an inch. Go at an angle if you want to look all fancy, but I prefer slicing straight on.

Crank your stove till you reach a rolling boil, keeping in mind you don't have to wait for the water to boil to add kielbasa. I know some folks like to time each step when it comes to the Low Country Boil dance, but I prefer freestyle.

After about 15 minutes, the water should be boiling nicely. If it's not, you need a new stove. Drop in the kielbasa (if you haven't already) and let it roll as you prep the onions and corn.

When the boil cranks back up, add the new potatoes. I said don't peel, but if you want to add a little designer touch, take a veggie peeler and nick off a sliver or two of each tater.

It will either look really cool, or like you dropped them on the back steps as you were running from the neighbor's dog.

Peel off the papery skin of the red and sweet onions. With that sharp knife you've grown to know and love, slice the onions into quarters. They'll fall apart plenty when they cook, much like a high school relationship.

Slice the lemons into halves and drop 'em in the pot. As many as you want, really. At least 6 or so. Let all this boil and roll together for at least 15 minutes before adding the corn, then let it go for about 5–7 minutes, stirring once or twice. Now, how do you know when it's time to dump the payload?

That's easy.

A. The kielbasa is floating and it's puffy, like the Magic Dragon, who lives by the sea. He also frolics, unlike most dragons.

B. The new potatoes are firm but soft to the touch, like poking a stale marshmallow.

C. As for the corn, I truly don't think you can overcook it, unless you fall asleep on your kitchen floor and wake up to the smell of burnt popcorn.

That is it, my friend. The stock of your Low Country Boil is *done*. You can either turn off the stove and drain what you've got or serve straight from the pot. I like it straight from the pot. You get more flavor that way, and the kielbasa stays nice and juicy till the last guest goes home.

Assuming, of course, they ever do.

BEAUTIFULLY BOILED SHRIMP (FROGMORE STEW'S FINAL STEP)

- 7 TO 8 POUNDS OF STRAIGHT-OUT-OF-THE NET MEDIUM-SIZED SHRIMP, ABOUT A 26-30 COUNT.
- DECENT-SIZED POT. THIS IS FOR BOILING THE SHRIMP, AND NOTHING ELSE. *AND NEVER THE TWAIN SHALL MEET*, FOR YOU KIPLING BUFFS.
- SLOTTED GATHERING SPOON FOR TESTING THE DONENESS OF THE GOODIES AFTER TIME WELL-SPENT IN THE BIG-ASS POT.
- COLANDER FOR DRAINING THE LOW COUNTRY BOIL—OPTIONAL.
- COLANDER FOR DRAINING THE SHRIMP—NOT OPTIONAL.

PREPARATION

While everything is rolling down the boiling alley, add a little water to your shrimp pot and turn up the heat. But before you do, let me offer a few trade secrets.

Shrimp are fairly moist by nature (who knew?) and can actually be boiled in little to no water, especially if you are only boiling for two. Just drop 'em in the pot, turn the eye on medium, stand close watch, and stir. Another neat trick is to boil shrimp in just a few fingers of water, a shot of white vinegar, and a couple solid shakes of Old Bay Seasoning, stirring as you go, as shrimp cook damn fast.

I repeat—shrimp cook damn fast. Overcooked is overkill and put Men at Work out of a job.

As for which method is preferred, I'm cool with either. Just don't drown 'em (you may recall the same goes for collard greens). This makes you look like a landlubber, and me a no-teaching mother.

When shrimp are done their meat turns opaque, almost cotton ball-white where the head used to be, and the shell becomes a faded orange sunset. Soon as you see these colors, pour the shrimp into the colander and dust on some Old Bay Seasoning. The reason I love this little touch is that when you peel the shrimp the Old Bay sticks to your fingers, and you can't help but welcome a little kick on the lips, tongue, and taste buds. And who doesn't love a little kick?

Wouldn't be life without it!

CLUBHOUSE FRIED SHRIMP

(SERVES 8-10)

─────────────

Shrimp could just as easily have been fried in the caddy house at Augusta as in the clubhouse (we certainly had enough grease to do the job!), but that tasty crustacean never saw hide nor hair of our worn wooden tables. Not that we didn't have it good in the eats department inside those old cinder block walls—we most certainly did. If I could ever go back in time to those palate-pleasing caddy yard meals, there isn't a chew I would change.

Especially if it included this one.

INGREDIENTS AND TOOLS OF THE TRADE

- Cooking oil, preferable soybean, peanut, or a blend thereof.
- FryDaddy or electric fryer.
- 5 pounds of medium-sized shrimp, peeled and deveined.
- Your old friend Mr. Sharp knife.
- Decent-sized bowl, plate, or pan for breading and tossing the soon-to-be-butterflied shrimp.
- Old Bay Seasoning.
- House-Autry 1812 seafood breading. Zatarain's is good stuff, too.
- Slotted strainer spoon.
- Paper towels.
- Large paper-toweled plate for when you pull the fried shrimp out of the fryer to be drained and patted.
- Lemons for drizzling onto the finished product.

PREPARATION

Pour the oil in the FryDaddy up to the line that lets you know: Hey, that's enough. Let the oil heat until it's good and hot. By now you should know what that means.

If you don't, God help us.

As the oil makes its way to Fahrenheit 451 (looks like we're burning books after all!), take your sharp knife and nick a little slice on the top side of each peeled shrimp, about halfway down from head to tail. This is a little caddy trick of the trade. The shrimp will now cook faster, more evenly. This is known as butterflying, not to be confused with dragon flying, where you live and die in a 24-hour span.

That's no way to run a rodeo, let me tell you.

Place the butterflied shrimp in the decent-sized bowl, plate, or pan. Sprinkle on a little Old Bay, letting that seafood saving grace rain down like moonlight through the pines. Now add the House-Autry and flippity-flop the shrimp around in the breading until lightly coated—light enough to still see the shrimp meat. We're not making hushpuppies here. Be sure and shake off the excess breading before frying, but there shouldn't really be any, unless you spilled your beer into the bowl.

When the oil is cracklin' like Rosie, get on board and add a dozen or so breaded shrimp. I use my hands. So can you, just be careful. If you're reckless as Evel Knievel, use your slotted spoon to ease 'em into the fryer, less you burn down not only the house but the skin off your hands and fingers. If you think shrimp *boil* fast, you ain't seen nothing yet, my friend. Shrimp fry faster than shots dropped on the 12th at Augusta!

Just 45 seconds and you're done—60, tops.

After a minute max, scoop out the shrimp. Put 'em on the paper-toweled plate, gently dabbing off any grease with the loose paper towel I know you have handy. Serve 'em hot, with lemons for drizzling on that flavor-enhancing juice (not that these shrimp need it—but I do love me some lemons). Don't worry—they'll cool down plenty by the time they reach the table.

And *that* is how we fry shrimp down South.

A BREATH OF FRESH AIR

It's the first week in February, with frost on the ground and a bite in the air. My main man is in town, a North Dakota gent who *winters* in Bemidji, Minnesota, of all places. Mr. B. hasn't worn a sweater since Coolidge was a boy. His idea of snow is a blizzard, and I don't mean the kind you get at Dairy Queen.

At Augusta, a February frost melts faster than Green Jacket dreams, and by 9 a.m. we find ourselves standing on the 1st tee, ready to roll. *First thing smoking*, as we caddies called it.

First on the tee, so set my ass free!

There were and still are no tee times at Augusta—it's first come, first serve, and the only way to get in line is to leave a ball against the wooden tee marker the night before. For Mr. B's group, this is overkill. Even though it has the makings of a beautiful winter day, at this ever-warming moment we are the only group on the tee. Only group on the entire grounds, hard as that is to believe.

Where the heck *is* everybody?

I'll ask that question often during my four seasons of hiking the hills at Augusta National. With the exception of October, when the club reopens for play, and early March until the season ends in May, Augusta is as much ghost town as it is O.K. Corral.

Today, my man Mr. B. has his group of regulars in tow, three NYC boys who love the game in all the right ways. The caddies are regulars, too, with Tip Light of sausage biscuit fame, loveable Larry —who subs for Donahue or California when the alarm clocks don't go off (Donahue's apparently did), and me. And while Mr. B. likes our group of caddies just fine and pays us well above The Rule, he's made it quite clear that if any of us show up one more time with alcohol on our breath there will be hell to pay, and our fired-asses won't have the money to do it.

157

Well, a caddy showing up to work without alcohol on his breath is like a golf club without a grip!

While there are many ways to play hide and go seek with booze breath, what happened next was new to even me, and I thought I'd seen it all in the caddy world. Who knew pine needles were so darn versatile?

Having made it through the first hole leaking oil like a funny car and smelling like the corner of 12th Street and Lynch, Larry knew his footsteps were numbered if he didn't do something about his breath, so thick with the smell of malt liquor you could walk to the moon on it.

After handing the Taylor Made Burner driver to his player and mumbling something about *right of center, Boss, and draw it like Picasso* (which, if you've ever actually *seen* a Picasso, means everything but a straight line), Larry slips down the left side of the fairway, jumping like a pogo stick every few steps, flailing his arms like he's swatting piñatas.

What in the hell?

I move in closer to see what's going on—with Larry, there ain't no telling.

Larry stops abruptly and turns to face me with chipmunk cheeks, a handful of chomped pine needles, and a shit-eating grin. He makes an oval with his lips and breathes out, gentle as a cooing dove.

I'll be damned.

Larry looks back as Mr. B. bunts his drive down the middle and shuffles off the tee box in our general direction. Larry pats me on the shoulder and winks.

"Watch and learn, White Boy. Watch and learn."

I follow at an educated distance as Larry falls in step with Mr. B.

"Beautiful day, ain't it?" says Larry, a hand-sweeping gesture like a jumpsuited Mufasa, as if to say, *One day, all of this will be yours.*

"Why, yes, Larry. It most certainly is. Looks like we've got the whole place to ourselves, too." Mr. B. stops walking, and there's a faraway look in his eyes, as if life has come to a sudden end. "Just one of the many things I love about Augusta, and what I love most about coming down here in February. There's just *nobody* here." Mr. B. smiles and wipes his hand on brown corduroys, the cuffs damp with dew. "In fact, Polly from the pro shop just told me there are no more groups on the grounds but us until after—until after—" Mr. B. stops speaking, twitches his nose like a rabbit.

"Until after *what*, Mr. B.?"

"Say, what's that smell?"

"Well, I can promise you it ain't alcohol," says Larry. "I'm dry as a cotton swab."

Another twitch of the nose by Mr. B.

"No, it's not alcohol. Why, it—it smells like Christmas!"

"I'll be damned," says Larry, blowing out air like a beluga whale. "It *does* smell like Christmas. Reminds me of when I was a kid, and Granddaddy would take us out to Uncle Remus's Christmas Tree Farm, and we'd cut down our own tree with nothing but pocket knives and gumption."

"Yes!" exclaims Mr. B., quite pleased with the discovery. "That's *exactly* what I'm smelling. Fresh cut Christmas trees."

"Well, you know Augusta, Mr. B. There ain't nothing they can't do out here."

Mr. B. smiles and nods his ball-capped head, his nose offering up one last twitch. I hand him his 4-wood, an old oil-hardened MacGregor with four screws in the face plate. He grips it like Hogan and stripes it like a zebra. I watch in amazement, but not surprise—my 74-year-old Jack Frost can still play a little—as his ball bounds down the fairway towards the green.

Larry starts singing, blowing out Christmas with every breath. Let's wish him a merry one, shall we?

CADDY HOUSE ASS-SAVING CHEWING GUM

(FEEDS ONE)

INGREDIENTS AND TOOLS OF THE TRADE

- LOBLOLLY PINE NEEDLES, THE FRESHER THE BETTER.
- DECENT VERTICAL LEAP.
- PENCHANT FOR SAP.
- STRONG SET OF MOLARS.
- SPECIAL PLACE IN YOUR HEART FOR CHRISTMAS.

PREPARATION

When no one is looking, break from your group and head to the nearest loblolly pine. Fear not, they're everywhere. Augusta's grounds crew tends to trim the lower hanging branches to the nubbins, so this is where a decent vertical leap will serve you well. Position yourself under a loblolly pine with reachable branches. Jump like a pogo stick and reach for the sky, grabbing a handful of needles as you make your way down. Fold the needles like you would a love note, then slip the Evergreen contraband into your mouth like it's God's own Juicy Fruit.

Be sure and save a piece for Santa.

A CUISINE LONG
MISINTERPRETED

I can't speak for other parts of the USA (I can't speak Italian, either) but in the South, spaghetti has taken on a life of its own since the moment it set foot on the southern steps of North America. Knock on any door in any state from Virginia to Georgia, knuckles trickling down like scuppernong vines so you hit Tennessee, Alabama, and the Carolinas, and you'll get 1,000 different answers to Italy's most misinterpreted contribution to kick-ass cuisine.

I say misinterpreted for two reasons. One, everybody thinks they can make spaghetti simply by opening a jar that says it's so and adding a few favorite ingredients like mushrooms, ground beef, and an overall lack of understanding.

The second reason is spaghetti, by Italian standards and design, is an *appetizer*—like burgundy escargot or bruschetta—simply the first of many courses that await the palate should you be lucky enough to dine in an authentic Italian restaurant. (I've often wondered if authentic restaurants refer to themselves as such? Let's hope not.)

Especially if that restaurant were located in New York City, hidden like a Christmas gift on the Upper East Side, closer to the York side of things, rubbing shoulders with the ebb and flow of the mighty East River. Not sure if the East River actually ebbed while on my watch, but I do know it flowed, and watching her waters flow from my vantage point of concrete banks and bolted-down park benches gave an odd sense of comfort to my brief run for the McCann-Erickson roses as a copywriter during the summer and winter of '93.

They say that youth is wasted on the young. Well, not on me, it wasn't!

Ah, the McCann days. I'd been given the nod to go work as a pen to paper man for fabled *Truth Well Told* McCann Erickson, the largest advertising agency in the world. During my days there—thanks to a lovely young woman who worked on Wall Street and was a wickedly beautiful blend of southern Alabama and second-generation Italian—I quickly learned what Italians mean when they ask, "Would you like some spaghetti?"

"This is incredible," I say, looking across a dark, wooden table through flickering candlelight. This place looks like it gave birth to Sophia Loren, Lollobrigida, and Isabella Rossellini, all in the same day. I can only imagine what sort of genes have been passed down through the generations of spaghetti that are about to walk through those batwing kitchen doors!

As if shot from a cannon, a gazelle-like waiter brings out menus, bulbous glasses of red house wine (when you're as broke as I am *any* wine is a good wine, especially when there's lots of it), and slides all four onto the table with an Italian accent thick as eggplant. I eagerly open my menu, eyes racing to the entrees. Spaghetti. Spaghetti. I don't see my favorite dish anywhere. There's osso bucco alla Milanese, ribollita, even lasagna, but none of my mama's spaghetti.

"It's over here," says Wall Street, pointing to the appetizer column of my menu. There's no real description to speak of. Just two words: marinara, alfredo.

Either, or.

"Oh, gotcha," I say, though I really want to say "What the hell? I'm in a for-real Italian restaurant on the Upper East Side and this is their idea of spaghetti? I could see this at the Olive Garden back home, but not here, not in New York."

I try not to feel as lost as I surely must appear, so I buck up and order the spaghetti marinara, along with fried anchovy stuffed zucchini blossoms, chicken parmesan, and Amaretti cookies for dessert (not that I have any plans for being hungry by then).

Holy shit, this is a lot of food!

We're in the midst of small talk—my minimum wage salary vs her monster commissioned one—when my spaghetti arrives, as if dropped from the sky. Wall Street ordered mussels, littleneck clams bathed in a white wine sauce that looks, and smells, heavenly. God's bathwater has been drawn.

Wall Street pulls her bowl of mussels close for what I am guessing is a better look. I stare down into my plate of spaghetti like a third grader at a love note. If I look long and hard enough, maybe the name I'm seeing will change from mine to someone else's.

"Something wrong?"

I'm so dumbfounded, I can't tell who's asking—Wall Street or the waiter.

"Oh, no. I mean, uh, well, yes. I mean, no. Sort of."

"Not what you expected?"

I poke the spaghetti with my fork, even though my mama taught me *never* to do that at the dinner table, especially not someone else's. But mama's not here.

"Are you OK?" Wall Street asks. She tilts her head as if she knows the answer.

Oh, how I want to say yes as I stare into the red sauce and noodles that is my Italian spaghetti. Mama's voice is in my ear: Shugah, if you can't think of anything nice to say, don't say anything at all. Now *that* I can do.

Still, I don't know whether to bless this meal or pray for it.

So I dig into my spaghetti. It's surprisingly damn good, this spaghetti. The sauce is, anyway.

It's an eclectic mix of diced and crushed tomatoes, with hints of fresh basil and parsley bits that float inside the sauce like a game of hide and seek. But the noodles are thick, like swollen coffee stirrers, and snappy to the bite. Al dente, I hear her say.

More like Al the dentist!

I think I just chipped a tooth.

I'm kidding, of course, in the way you might kid about a roller coaster ride that you swear made you soil your skivvies, when deep down you loved every bowel-emptying second of it. I gotta admit this marinara sauce is one for the ages, as if the angels (whose hair is still on their head and not on my plate) made it just for me. It's rich as Uncle Scrooge, with fireworks of flavor I can't quite define. But it belongs on a pizza, not in spaghetti. Or in this case, *on* spaghetti, since that word describes the pasta, not the dish. At least it does to me.

Although I often talk about that Italian meal with Wall Street as one of the best I've ever had and one I'll never forget, I can't help but think how my life might've turned out if Italy made spaghetti caddy yard style. I also can't help but smile knowing my life's pot is a melting one, and every time I make spaghetti I think back on that New York night, the Italian restaurant on the corner of 81st and 3rd (or was it 83rd and York?), the green-eyed woman of Wall Street (I hope her life worked out—she deserves happiness), and the fireworks of flavor that wrapped around my fork as I ate my *first*, and *last*, authentic Italian meal.

Buon appetito!

THE BEST SPAGHETTI
THIS SIDE OF THE BOOT

(Serves 12–16)

———————

INGREDIENTS AND TOOLS OF THE TRADE

- That good-sized pot that you now love like family. This is for the spaghetti sauce.
- Sharp knife.
- Olive oil cooking spray.
- 1 jar Paul Newman's marinara.
- 1 jar Paul Newman's basil marinara.
- 3 jars Paul Newman's Sockarooni.
- 2 cans Del Monte garlic and onion diced tomatoes.
- 2 cans Del Monte Italian stewed tomatoes.
- 2 cans Del Monte original diced tomatoes.
- 3–6 tricolored peppers. Sauté and microwave 'em first to save a step and a stitch in time. They'll be so good and tender when you're done, the kids won't even know they're in there.
- 1 bell pepper.
- 2 Vidalia onions.
- Microwaveable bowl.
- Decent-sized pan for sautéing.
- Kitchen Basics chicken stock.
- Sprinkles of celery salt.
- Dashes of McCormick's lemon pepper.
- Ground pepper.

- DASHES OF MCCORMICK'S MEDITERRANEAN GARLIC SALT.
- 32 OUNCES WHITE MUSHROOMS. WHOLE IS PREFERRED IF YOU HAVE TIME, BUT PRE-SLICED IS OK.
- PROPER BUTTER, LIKE OLIVIO OR KERRYGOLD.
- COUPLE CLOVES OF GARLIC, OR THE ALREADY PRESSED, SOLD IN A JAR KIND. I'M COOL WITH EITHER.
- BIG SPLASH OF GRUET BLANC DE NOIRS, WHITE WINE, OR DOMESTIC BEER. STAY AWAY FROM DARK BEERS, SUCH AS GUINNESS. WE AIN'T MAKING CORNED BEEF AND CABBAGE HERE.
- DASHES OF DRIED OREGANO, PARSLEY, ONION.
- A FEW BAY LEAVES.
- SOY SAUCE.
- WORCESTERSHIRE SAUCE.
- 2 POUNDS OF 73/27 GROUND BEEF.
- PROPER SKILLET WITH A LID THAT FITS.
- OLIVE OIL, BUT JUST A FEW DROPS.
- DECENT-SIZED POT FOR BOILING THE ANGEL HAIR PASTA.
- BOX OF ANGEL HAIR PASTA.
- HAVARTI.
- A LITTLE TIME ON YOUR HANDS—THIS TAKES ABOUT AN HOUR TO PREPARE, BUT IT IS WORTH EVERY TICK OF THE CLOCK.

PREPARATION

Spray your new best friend the good-sized pot with cooking spray. Add a couple jars of Paul Newman's Basil and Marina spaghetti sauce, the Sockarooni, too and a couple cans of stewed *and* diced tomatoes: both garlic and onion and original flavors. Turn the burner on medium low. Spaghetti sauce can scorch if you crank up the heat too high, too fast, or too long.

Get to chopping. We've already gone over how, so dice up the peppers and onions the best you can. Small is good—about the size of a pencil eraser. Be sure when you dice the peppers you clean them first. By clean, I mean just clean out the seeds. The white lining bit that looks a little like that stitching? Leave that.

Put the peppers and onions in a decent-sized microwaveable bowl. Add enough chicken stock to get 'em just below floating. Sprinkle on celery salt, lemon pepper, ground pepper, Worcestershire sauce, and garlic salt. Pop the veggies in the microwave and look for the "dinner plate" button. It may also say "reheat." These are magic microwave buttons. These buttons heat your food, as opposed to cooking it. You almost *never* want to cook anything in a microwave, unless it's popcorn.

Repeat this dinner plate step 2 to 3 times, stirring at each new beginning. You may need to add a little more chicken stock, which is fine. I prefer to refer to it as store-bought au jus.

Or, liquid gold.

If you're happy with what you see, slide the bowl back into the micro and shut the door. Remember, the microwave and stove are the tightest sealed doors in the house, except for the front door when the wife locks you out. (Though that would never happen. Right, darling? Darling? Oh, damn. My key's not working!)

Next are the 'shrooms. White, as I mentioned, or Portabella. Portabellas are an excellent addition to the spore family but a bit more expensive, and unless you cook 'em up when they're fresh as a daisy, their flavor can be a bit overwhelming, like perfume at a Baptist funeral. If you like overwhelmingly flavored mushrooms and you've got some week-old portabellas in the back of the fridge, then my friend, it's your lucky day.

If you bought the mushrooms whole, slice 'em with that very sharp knife of yours. Thin or thick, whichever you prefer. Keep in mind, at least in my experience with the spore family, most folks like 'em thin.

Turn the burner on medium and add a dab of butter and a heaping spoonful of pressed garlic to your decent-sized pan. Toss in the sliced mushrooms, and pour in a little beer, white wine, or Gruet. Sprinkle in some seasonings like the dried oregano, parsley, and onion. Slip in the bay leaves. Add the soy and Worcestershire sauce, too. I go all in, myself. Stir up the goodness. It'll take about 15 to 20 minutes to get the 'shrooms just right. And by just right, I mean tasting like mushroom heaven. Only way I know for sure is to taste one, so be sure you do just that.

Now comes the fun part (though if you're like me and you love cooking and a good story, then it's *all* fun).

In that big pot where the jars of Newman's Basil, Marinara, Sockarooni and the various flavors of Del Monte tomatoes have slowly been heating, start adding stuff. More sauce, more tomatoes, all the peppers and onions, the au jus, too. Leave about six inches of room from the surface to the top of the pot. The ground beef, and the juice of the ground beef, is next.

This, for you meat lovers, is the hub of the spaghetti wheel. If you're not digging the meat, that's cool. You're still in the process of making some pretty amazing spaghetti sauce.

But if you *are* digging the meat, go back to the large pan where the 'shrooms are sunbathing in seasoning and add the ground beef. All of it, if it'll fit. If you can marry the flavor of ground beef and 'shrooms, your spaghetti sauce will be the better for it.

Stir here and there, but not like some desperate game show contestant (you want some chunks in the meat if you can), as you season the mushroom-meaty goodness. Just dashes, of course, but add whatever you like, whatever you deem fit or necessary. Stir the browning beef. I use a spoon, but I know some folks dig the spatula. It'll take about 8 to 10 minutes (if you think I'm counting, think again) to get the meat browned and where you want it. The mushrooms, if they're still in the pan with the ground beef, are on autopilot, just soaking up flavor in waves.

OK, time to put a ribbon on this curl.

Here, you can go two ways, and while I prefer one over the other, I'm quite cool with either. My preferred way to add seasoned ground beef and mushrooms to spaghetti sauce is to simply add it all. Juice included. Yes, a little of that juice is also grease. But it's good grease, and what this squeaky wheel wants. But if you want to drain the ground beef and 'shrooms before adding them to the sauce, that's fine.

Now, stir up what you've got. The whole house should smell nothing short of fabulous. Take a spoon and taste your hard work. Does it need anything? I doubt it.

After all this has been rolling for about an hour or so, you should be in pretty good shape. Turn the burner down low, put the lid on your pot, and let the sauce, *your* sauce, coast.

Now for the pasta.

Get the water boiling, adding a splash of olive oil as you do. Yes, I know some chefs say don't add oil to the water because if you do the sauce won't soak into the noodles.

Since when does sauce soak into noodles?

When it's rolling, rolling, rolling, keep them wagons rolling and add the box of angel hair. All of it. When it's cooked, you'll be surprised how far one box of angel hair goes. Like one of those new high-tech golf balls, even if you've got a low-tech swing.

After about five minutes of steady boiling, the angel hair should be ready. Now *here's* the secret to perfect pasta.

Leave it in the pot.

Drain a little of the water but leave enough to just cover the noodles. This keeps 'em moist, just the right texture, and sticky-free. Like duty free, but without all the airport security checks and overpriced beverages.

OK, last little secret to an incredible plate of spaghetti.

I grew up on putting cheese on my spaghetti noodles before adding the sauce. Mozzarella we shredded ourselves was the cheese of choice when I was a young lad. These days, it's Havarti, which is as gooey when heated as it is mildly flavorful. If you've never tried putting Havarti on angel hair pasta before slathering on that some kind of amazing spaghetti sauce you just made, I highly recommend you do.

It's funny. I was once asked to pick up a few slices of Havarti during a grocery store run, asked if I had ever heard of it. And to top it all off, even had it spelled out for me, one "Wheel of Fortune" letter at a time.

H-A-V-A-R-T-I.

Stay in school, kids.

LOCALLY FAMOUS AND WORLD-RENOWNED GREEN JACKET SALAD

(AND THE DRESSING THAT MAKES IT SO DAMN GOOD!)

(SERVES 8-10)

———————

There's a story behind every great recipe, just like behind every successful man there's a great woman. The Green Jacket Salad is no exception.

It was thanks to love that this recipe found its way to me, and now I bring it to you. With love, of course.

INGREDIENTS AND TOOLS OF THE TRADE

- 8 TABLESPOONS VEGETABLE OIL.
- 3 TO 4 NICE-SIZED RIPE TOMATOES, FOR BLENDING.
- 12 TABLESPOONS RED WINE VINEGAR.
- 4 TEASPOONS DRIED OREGANO.
- 4 TEASPOONS LAWRY'S SEASONED SALT.
- 2 TEASPOONS ACCENT.
- 2 TEASPOONS FRESH OR DRIED PARSLEY.
- BLENDER—DOESN'T HAVE TO BE FANCY. COULD BE A LUCKY YARD SALE FIND. JUST NEEDS TO BE ABLE TO PURÉE.
- A COUPLE MASON JARS OR SPAGHETTI SAUCE JARS FOR SERVING AND STORING THE DRESSING. BOTH ARE PERFECT, THOUGH CHANCES ARE YOU WON'T FILL EITHER TO THE TOP UNLESS YOU DOUBLE THE DRESSING.
- 2 HEADS OF ICEBERG LETTUCE.
- COUPLE HANDFULS OF CHERRY TOMATOES FOR SLICING AND ADDING TO THE SALAD.
- 1 BAG OF PITA CHIPS. HOMEMADE ROCKS, BUT THERE ARE SOME GOOD STORE-BOUGHT

ONES OUT THERE, LIKE STACY'S.
- DECENT-SIZED MIXING BOWL.
- SPOON FOR TASTE-TESTING.
- DISH TOWEL—THIS COULD GET MESSY.
- BEACH TOWEL, IN CASE YOU FORGET TO PUT THE BLENDER LID ON TIGHT BEFORE YOU FLIP THE PURÉE SWITCH.
- COLD PLATES FOR SERVING (REFRIGERATE THEM NOW, IF YOU CAN).

PREPARATION

Although this recipe includes what just might be the best salad dressing to ever jump on a bed of lettuce, it is some kinda easy to make. To start, all the seasonings, oil, vinegar, and the four nice-sized tomatoes go in the blender. Drop 'em in, stir 'em up, snap on the lid. Put your hand firmly on that lid, like a mean kid with a jack in the box, or the shit won't be the *only* thing to hit the fan.

Flip the purée switch and let it do its thing. Let it whir and purr for 10 to 15 seconds, then taste test the dressing, keeping in mind this is a work in progress. What does it need? Another tomato? Little more red wine vinegar? Probably. Should be good on the others, unless you want to dash in a touch more oregano. Now, blend again, taste again. You'll know when it's right.

It's like falling in love. You'll just know. And when you do, take that blender full of the world's best dressing and pour it into the mason jars. You should come fairly close to filling each one up, but it's OK if you don't.

Chop the lettuce and tomatoes, placing them in a large salad bowl. Add the pita chips. The original recipe calls for homemade pita chips, and you can certainly make them if you like, but pita chips ain't what makes this salad so magical. It's the *dressing*; the very dressing you just made in that forgotten blender hiding in your cabinet. Well, I say hide no more!

With the salad where you want it, add that magical dressing and toss it like a baseball. Kidding. I have no idea why they call it "tossing" when you mix salad and dressing.

Just mix it up, like a rugby scrum.

Now pull those cold plates out of the refrigerator, add the Green Jacket Salad and serve immediately. Why serve on refrigerated plates? I don't have a clue. But I do know it's the last rung on the ladder that takes the Green Jacket Salad into the stratosphere.

If the sky truly *is* the limit, guess where we're going?

AUGUSTA'S CLUBHOUSE ICE CREAM, WITH VARIATIONS ON THE THEME

(SERVES PLENTY)

It was the best of times, it was the simplest of times. It certainly wasn't the worst of times. And even if it was, there ain't nothing that a bowl of homemade clubhouse ice cream can't fix.

INGREDIENTS AND TOOLS OF THE TRADE FOR CLUBHOUSE VANILLA ICE CREAM

- 24 EGG YOLKS.
- 2 VANILLA BEANS, CUT LENGTHWISE. SCRAPE OUT THE SEEDS.
- 2 1/4 CUPS OF SUGAR.
- ELECTRIC MIXER, UNLESS YOU HAVE THE HANDS OF SUPERMAN OR ELASTIGIRL.
- 2 QUARTS OF WHOLE MILK.
- 1 QUART OF CREAM.
- 1 TEASPOON OF SALT.
- GOOD-SIZE MIXING BOWL.
- GOOD-SIZE POT FOR BOILING THE GOODS.
- ICE CREAM MAKER, OR CHURN FOR STORING FREEZER-BOUND ICE CREAM.

PREPARATION

Strike up the band and sound the alarm. I've cited *actual* measurements for this one! Well, when it comes to making frozen things frozen and taste like they're supposed to taste, estimating is not an option.

177

Step 1: Combine those 24 egg yolks, vanilla beans, and enough sugar to sweeten a couple gallons of grandma's tea in a mixing bowl. Whip it all together in your electric mixer till it's thick and light. (Sounds like jumbo shrimp.)

Step 2: Pour the milk, cream, and salt into the pot and bring everything to a rolling boil.

Step 3: Add your boiled mixture of milk, cream, and salt to the thick and light mix of eggs and sugar ONE CUP AT A TIME, STIRRING AS YOU GO. Otherwise, forget it.

Step 4: Thoroughly chill the mixture from step 3. Put that goodness in your fridge and don't take it out until it's nice and cold, like your favorite beer after mowing the yard.

Step 5: Pour the chilled goodness into an ice cream maker or churn. Freeze.

Step 6: Serve. First to yourself, then to your guests. Quality control is key.

INGREDIENTS AND TOOLS OF THE TRADE FOR SKITTLES ICE CREAM

- 24 EGG YOLKS.
- 2 VANILLA BEANS, CUT LENGTHWISE. SCRAPE OUT THE SEEDS.
- 2CUPS OF SUGAR. NOTICE I REMOVED ¼ CUP OF SUGAR. GUESS WHAT REPLACED IT?
- ELECTRIC MIXER, UNLESS YOU HAVE THE HANDS OF SUPERMAN OR ELASTIGIRL.
- GOOD-SIZE MIXING BOWL.
- 2 QUARTS OF WHOLE MILK.
- 1 QUART OF CREAM.
- 1 TEASPOON OF SALT.
- GOOD-SIZE POT FOR BOILING THE GOODS.
- 1 SHARE SIZE BAG OF SKITTLES. WOOT, WOOT!

PREPARATION

Are you serious? *Skittles* ice cream? Man, I've died and gone to heaven!

Step 1: Combine those 24 egg yolks, vanilla beans, and enough sugar (minus the ¼ cup) to sweeten a couple gallons of grandma's tea in a mixing bowl. Whip it all together in your electric mixer till it's thick and light.

Step 2: Pour the milk, cream, and salt into the pot and bring everything to a rolling boil.

Step 3: Add your boiled mixture of milk, cream, and salt to the thick and light mix of eggs and sugar ONE CUP AT A TIME, STIRRING AS YOU GO. Pour in that share size bag of Skittles, stirring until they dissolve.

Step 4: Thoroughly chill the mixture from step 3. Put that goodness in your fridge and don't take it out until it's nice and cold, like your favorite beer hidden in the back of the patio fridge.

Step 5: Pour the chilled goodness into an ice cream maker or churn. Freeze.

Step 6: Serve. First to yourself, then to your guests. Quality control is key.

INGREDIENTS AND TOOLS OF THE TRADE FOR MINT-BASIL CHOCOLATE CHIP ICE CREAM

- 24 EGG YOLKS.
- 2 ¼ CUPS OF SUGAR.
- 2 VANILLA BEANS, CUT LENGTHWISE. SCRAPE OUT THE SEEDS.
- GOOD-SIZE MIXING BOWL.
- ELECTRIC MIXER, UNLESS YOU HAVE THE HANDS OF SUPERMAN OR ELASTIGIRL.
- 2 QUARTS OF WHOLE MILK.
- 1 QUART OF CREAM.
- 1 TEASPOON OF SALT.
- GOOD-SIZE POT FOR BOILING THE GOODS.
- 30 LEAVES OF FRESH MINT.
- 10 MEDIUM-SIZED BASIL LEAVES. I BET YOUR NEIGHBOR'S GARDEN HAS PLENTY.
- YOUR FAVORITE CHOCOLATE CHIPS.
- BLENDER.

PREPARATION

Perfect for watching the Kentucky Derby after a morning round at Augusta, this mint-basil chocolate chip ice cream will have you digging in your closet for that Derby fascinator or pink seersucker suit faster than Reba McEntire with a wardrobe change!

Step 1: Combine those 24 egg yolks, vanilla beans, and enough sugar to sweeten a couple gallons of grandma's tea in a mixing bowl. Whip it all together in your electric mixer till it's thick and light.

Step 2: Pour the milk, cream, and salt into the pot and bring everything to a rolling boil.

Step 3: Add your boiled mixture of milk, cream, and salt to the thick and light mix of eggs and sugar ONE CUP AT A TIME, STIRRING AS YOU GO. Otherwise, forget it.

Step 4: Add 30 leaves of fresh mint and 10 medium-size basil leaves to one cup of ice cream base (which you made during Step 3) and blend in the blender. Add to base and mix to combine.

Step 5: Chill the mixture from step 3 thoroughly. Put that goodness in your fridge and don't take it out until it's nice and cold, like your favorite beer hidden in the back of the patio fridge.

Step 6: Pour the chilled goodness into an ice cream maker or churn. Freeze.

Step 7: After freezing, fold in as many chocolate chips as you like.

Step 8: Serve. First to yourself, then to your guests. Quality control is key.

À LA CARTE: MY BRUSH WITH THE HALL OF FAME

During my four seasons as an Augusta National caddy, I learned many things that before I donned the white jumpsuit weren't even on my radar: To *remember* the greens, not read them. Knowing when to speak and when to hush my mouth. The art of casual grazing.

Why let the cows have all the fun?

As an Augusta caddy, I was a professional snacker—no caddy could do it better. The pockets on my caddy suit were well-water-deep. I could jam in my hands and you could barely see elbows. Yet my pockets were always chock full of a wide and wild variety of caddy house cuisine. You name it, I had it in there.

Deep fried porkchops, double-wrapped in wax paper to ward off dripping grease. Fried chicken sandwiches on squishy white bread, bone-in, double-wrapped for the same reason. A tinfoil-wrapped sausage biscuit from breakfast entrepreneur Tip Light Johnson (sometimes they were a buck apiece, depending on Tip's mood and the thickness of the patties, but for the guttural punch they packed they were worth twice the price). Sausage dogs, hold the hot sauce, lest it seeps through your jumpsuit and stains your thighs like a bleeding Sharpie.

The ever-present boiled egg, unpeeled and unabridged. Lay's potato chips and Nip Chee crackers. Butter beans consumed long before I left that morning's caddy yard. Grape sodas to wash it all down; one for the yard and one for the road.

It was in this condition—a walking snack bar—that I first met Daniel Constantine Marino, Jr. NFL superstar, Hall of Famer, and the first QB to pass for over 5,000 yards (this was 1984, when the NFL was still largely a rushing league).

When I was caddying at Augusta, I was the type of caddy who would introduce myself first thing, not wait for my player to start in first with small talk, or a silence that hung like bats in a cave.

"Hi, I'm Tripp," I'd say, offering my hand. If they came back, "Hi, Tripp. I'm Mr. Marino," then it was Tripp and Mr. Marino. But if he came back "Hi, Tripp. I'm Dan," well, then by God you're Dan and I'm Tripp. This Hall of Famer was most definitely a Dan, and the simple fact he introduced himself as such made us friends for life. Or at least for the next four and a half hours.

So we're tooling down the fairways of Augusta, Dan and I, shooting the shit and sharing stories of our lifetime achievements (or, in my case, my unachieved achievements). We were quite the combination: one of the greatest quarterbacks in the history of the NFL, and me, one of the greatest bull-shitters of the modern era. No wonder we got along so well. Player and caddy, caddy and player, strolling the fairways of Augusta without a care in the world. Dan and Tripp, Tripp and Dan.

It was as beautiful a moment as my young buck self had known, so beautiful I just had to ask Dan if perhaps he felt the same, for surely, he must.

So, after my last bite of my second bone sandwich, I walked over to Dan's bag and popped the question. It was late January, the southern winter temperature an absolute perfect 65°. The majestic loblollies swaying in the moment-making breeze, and with the exception of the Augusta member and Dan's agent, we had the golf course all to ourselves.

I just had to ask, so I did.

"Say there, Dan old friend. Sure is a beautiful day, ain't it?"

"Sure is, Tripp. You just now realizing it?"

"Oh, no," I say. "I've been feeling this way ever since the first tee. It's not every day you get to hang out with a Hall of Famer."

"I didn't know you were in the Hall of Fame, too," says Dan. He leans over like a buzzard and playfully pops my shoulder with his cantaloupe-sized fist.

"You know, Dan. I just can't imagine a better place to be than right here right now," I say, opening my arms to the sky. "Can you?"

Dan looks at me like I just sprouted 3-woods from my forehead, jams his hands on his hips like a substitute teacher who's not getting paid near enough to kick your ass. He leans in, all 6'5" of him (for the record, he's a *lot* bigger in real life than he looks on TV).

"Hell, yeah," he says, nodding his head like a bobbing doll collectable. I step back and crane my neck.

"Really?" I say. "Where?"

"The Super Bowl!"

CADDY YARD CHILI
AND THE DOGS THEY UNLEASH

(FEEDS 10-12)

Before you can unleash the Kraken, you must first identify the Kraken. In order to identify the Kraken, you must first make a big ol' pot of caddy yard chili (stay with me, friends), which isn't a whole lot different than making the mighty tasty caddy yard spaghetti from a few recipes back. Just get friendly with the cumin and tell the Italian seasonings to hit the road, mia amica.

For now, anyway.

Some folks might say *release* the Kraken, which means—in most dictionaries—to set free from restraint; to relieve from confinement or burden. As I'm sure you're quite aware by now, there are no burdens found here, and the only confinement I know is of some pretty tasty ingredients waiting inside bottles and cans, eager to put on a show.

Let's unleash the Kraken, shall we?

Curtains, please.

I can't recall my age, exactly, when I took my first bite of what would stay with me forever as the best chili I ever tasted. I only know I was old enough to realize what I was eating was *damn* good. Of course, had I said the word "damn" to describe a meal at my mama's kitchen table, a bar of soap would have been dessert. For those taking notes, Irish Spring tastes like shit.

As the years rolled by new ingredients rolled in, changing ever so slightly (how could they not?) from yellow corn to shoepeg corn, black beans to cannellini, garlic powder to garlic salt, but the handle of that hammer never changed. No matter the nail, there was always a memorable mix of cumin (shake it like a tractor wheel), proper chicken stock (pour to your heart's content), 73/27 ground beef (fresh as you can buy), zesty chili-style diced tomatoes (don't be fooled by the can), and the absolute biggest pot we could find. Good stock is good stock, no matter the dish. You should know that by now.

Oh, wait.

You do.

INGREDIENTS AND TOOLS OF THE TRADE

- 2 CANS OF RED KIDNEY BEANS.
- 2 CANS OF BLACK BEANS.
- 2 CANS OF CANNELLINI BEANS.
- COLANDER FOR DRAINING AND RINSING THE BEANS.
- 1 CAN ROTEL MEXICAN-STYLE DICED TOMATOES WITH LIME JUICE & CILANTRO.
- 1 CAN DEL MONTE MEXICAN TOMATOES.
- 2 CANS DEL MONTE DICED TOMATOES—ZESTY CHILI STYLE.
- 6 CANS OF DEL MONTE DICED OR STEWED TOMATOES. GO WITH ORIGINAL, CHILI, GARLIC AND ONION, GREEN PEPPERS, ONION AND BASIL.
- CHILI-MAKING KIT, SUCH AS WICKS FOWLER OR 2 ALARM. BOTH ARE EXCELLENT.
- 1 CAN WHITE SHOEPEG CORN. STAY AWAY FROM THE YELLOW KERNELS THAT LOOK LIKE A PIRATE'S VENEERS.
- ONE 32-OUNCE BOX OF KITCHEN BASICS CHICKEN STOCK OR KIRKLAND ORGANIC CHICKEN STOCK.
- GOOD-SIZED POT.
- COOKING SPRAY—FOR EITHER YOU OR THE POOR BASTARD THAT'S GOTTA WASH THE POT WHEN YOU'RE DONE.
- NONSTICK PAN.
- 4–5 POUNDS OF 73/27 GROUND BEEF. DO NOT GO 80/20—TOO DRY FOR MY TASTE. YOURS, TOO, I'D BET.
- TACO SEASONING. HOT OR MILD—UP TO YOU.
- FAJITA SEASONING.
- FRONTERA CILANTRO TACO SKILLET SAUCE.
- SEASONINGS—THE USUAL SUSPECTS SUCH AS GARLIC SALT, LEMON PEPPER, CELERY SALT, GROUND PEPPER.
- 4 GARLIC CLOVES, OR PRESSED GARLIC IN THE JAR.
- CUMIN.
- SOY SAUCE.
- WORCESTERSHIRE SAUCE.
- ONE 16-OUNCE LIGHT BEER.
- GRUET OR WHITE WINE—NO RED.
- 2 SWEET ONIONS.

- **FOUR TO SIX TRICOLORED PEPPERS.**
- **1 BELL PEPPER.**
- **1 PACKET OF CHICKEN GOYA.**
- **TRUSTY LADLE FOR SERVING.**

PREPARATION

OK, let's roll out some caddy yard chili!

Open all the cans of beans and drain, rinse, and rinse them again (even if they came already seasoned). In your good-sized pot with the burner on low, add all the canned tomatoes, and the chili kit—go easy on the chili powder; you can add more as you go along. Add the shoepeg corn, but don't drain.

Add the rinsed and drained beans, as well as the corn and chicken stock, and give it all a good stirring. Be careful on the heat so as not to scald. Whoever said a watched pot never boils needs to get a new stove.

In your favorite skillet, brown the ground beef, adding a ½ packet each of taco and fajita mix as you do. Dash in the additional seasonings—cumin, ground pepper, celery salt, garlic salt, and fresh crushed garlic. Keep in mind that a little cumin goes a long way but remember: some of us have further to go than others. As the meat browns, dash in the soy and Worcestershire.

Pour that tall boy cold one in your chili pot, if you haven't already polished it off. If no longer handy, white wine or champagne works, too. As does good old-fashioned water. Think a cup or so, but again, the amount is up to you, now that you know what the hell you're doing. You *do* know what the hell you're doing, don't you?

Of course you do.

Remember how you chopped, seasoned, and microwaved the onions, bell pepper, and tricolored peppers to make that kick-ass spaghetti sauce? Do that again for caddy yard chili, every simple step. Please note: there are *no* mushrooms in chili. To quote the late, great Augusta caddy yard philosopher Darrell "Nut" Chestnut, "Oh, no. *Never* that."

Stir the browned and seasoned ground beef until you're happy and satisfied with what you have. When you are, add in the microwaved onions and peppers and shake in a packet of chicken Goya. Stir. Let this go ten to fifteen minutes or so before tasting the meat.

Taste the meat.

If you find yourself smiling like Ronald McDonald in a Roy Rogers drive-through, pour that seasoned goodness into your simmering pot of chili stock. *All* of it. Do not drain a single drop of flavor. Just stir it all in with that ladle of yours. Let it coast on medium low, if time allows. I'm sure you could cook chili for what folks call long enough, but Father Time may have other plans.

And that, my dear friends, is it—caddy yard chili, from my house to yours.

Now, how 'bout them chili dogs (see page 189)?

KNIFE AND FORK CHILI DOGS

(FEEDS 8)

———————

While there are many ways to roll out a chili dog, there just might be none better than via the knife and fork modus operandi. Should you decide to swap out knife for spoon upon seeing this beauty hold court on your plate, I won't hold it against you.

Neither will the judge.

INGREDIENTS AND TOOLS OF THE TRADE

- THAT ROCKIN' HOMEMADE CHILI YOU JUST MADE (PAGE 185).
- MEDIUM POT FOR BOILING THE DOGS.
- ONE 32-OUNCE BOX OF KITCHEN BASICS CHICKEN STOCK. (OPTIONAL, BUT TRY IT AT LEAST ONCE BEFORE YOU CALL ME BAT SHIT CRAZY.)
- PACK OF HOT DOGS. YOUR CHOICE. I DIG BALL PARK, OSCAR MAYER, IN A PINCH CAROLINA PRIDE.
- PACK OF HOT DOG BUNS, ALSO YOUR CHOICE. BUT *PLEASE* DO NOT SCRIMP HERE, AS THERE IS INDEED SUCH A THING AS A CRAPPY HOT DOG BUN. IF THE PACK COSTS LESS THAN 2 BUCKS, EVEN ON SALE, DON'T BUY IT.
- TUPPERWARE LARGE ENOUGH TO HOLD 8 DOGS IN THEIR BUNS, PRIOR TO TOPPING WITH CADDY YARD CHILI. TIGHT SEAL IS A MUST. FOR THIS, I LOVE RUBBERMAID ESSENTIALS. BEST THERE IS.
- CONDIMENTS. I DON'T USE ANY. IF A PICTURE'S WORTH 1,000 WORDS, THIS CHILI IS *WAR AND PEACE.*
- CHEESE OF CHOICE. I'M OK IF YOU WANT TO ADD SOME, THOUGH YOU DON'T REALLY NEED IT. THAT SAID, MEXICAN BLEND, TACO BLEND, AND ALSO MY

BELOVED HAVARTI WILL COMPLEMENT THE CHILI DOGS NICELY.
- CERAMIC BOWLS OR SHALLOW, CERAMIC PLATES—IT'S GOING TO GET MESSY, IN A VERY GOOD WAY.
- KNIFE AND FORK. A SPOON WON'T HURT MY FEELINGS.
- LOTS OF PROPER NAPKINS, SUCH AS VANITY FAIR DINNER NAPKINS. COME ON, LIVE A LITTLE.

PREPARATION

Fill your pot about halfway with water, or, if you've taken me up on it, about half the container of chicken stock. It'll give it that little something extra if you do.

Either way, boil the dogs for 10 minutes, give or take. Depending on the brand, some can split like balsa wood if you go too long. As for the brand of dogs, like I said, your choice. I tend to go with what I grew up with, like Oscar Mayer Wieners, Ball Park, Carolina Pride.

You can always finish the dogs on the grill if you'd like to and have the time. It's damn hard to beat a grilled dog—no doubt about that. Either way, when the dogs are done to your liking, slide them one by one into the good buns (*please* tell me you bought some) and pop 'em in the Tupperware for a few minutes, clamping the lid shut. The heat from the just-boiled hot dogs will steam the buns, which to me makes the better even better, and that's saying a lot.

Now take the dogs and put them in the serving bowls, generously spooning on the chili, *your* caddy yard chili, as you take stock of the drooling faces anxiously awaiting the best chili dog this side of the Varsity. Be as generous with the napkins as you were with the chili, and for the love of all that's holy and sacred, save the plastic cutlery for the drive-through.

Promise?

N'AWLINS GUMBO, CADDY YARD STYLE

[SERVES 14-16]

Gumbo is the melting pot of all that we are.
—DONAHUE, long-time Augusta caddy, good friend, and resident caddy yard philosopher

INGREDIENTS AND TOOLS OF THE TRADE

- 8 STALKS CELERY, FINELY CHOPPED—CHOP THE LEAVES, TOO. DON'T TAKE 'EM OFF, THEY'RE GOOD!
- ½ CUP OF PARSLEY, FINELY CHOPPED—EASY TO JUST TOSS THE PARSLEY IN A COFFEE CUP AND CUT IT UP WITH KITCHEN SCISSORS. ITALIAN PARSLEY ROCKS.
- 3 FIST-SIZED ONIONS, ALSO FINELY CHOPPED. SWEET ONIONS ARE BEST, LIKE A VIDALIA OR SEASONAL SWEET. NO RED ONIONS HERE. WE'RE MAKING GUMBO, NOT LOW COUNTRY BOIL.
- BAG OR TRAY OF SWEET PEPPERS—IT'S CHEAPER TO GO TO A SAM'S OR COSTCO FOR THIS. BUT NO MATTER WHERE YOU GO, BE SURE TO GET THE TRICOLORED BELLS AND CHOP UP EVERY ONE OF THEM!
- 1 BELL PEPPER.
- 2–4 CLOVES OF GARLIC, MINCED. UP TO YOU HOW MANY—I USUALLY ROLL WITH 4, BUT I LOVE ME SOME GARLIC!
- COUPLE GRANDMA-GRABBING-ON-YOUR-CHEEKS PINCHES OF THYME.
- 2 POUNDS FROZEN OKRA—*IF* YOUR POT IS BIG ENOUGH. IF IT'S NOT, GO GET A BIGGER ONE. OKRA (MY SISTER AND I CALL IT "OKREE") IS KEY. THERE IS *NO* GUMBO WITHOUT OKRA.
- MIGHTY SHARP KNIFE, FOR HANDLING ALL OF THE ABOVE.
- THAT KICK-ASS WIRE WHISK FOR MAKING AND STIRRING THE ROUX.
- SOLID SPOON FOR STIRRING THE REST.
- ALL THE SEASONINGS THAT HAVE BEEN WITH US DURING THIS FUN-LOVING

FORAY OF RECIPES TO REMEMBER—AND MOST IMPORTANTLY, MAKE YOUR OWN. *ESPECIALLY* THE LEMON PEPPER.

- ONE BEER. NEEDS TO BE A DOMESTIC. IMPORTS CAN BE A BIT HEAVY.
- COOKING SPRAY.
- THAT BIG OL' POT I KNOW YOU NOW HAVE.
- 1 CUP OIL—I USUALLY USE CANOLA OR OLIVE, BUT REGULAR, *NOT* EXTRA VIRGIN.
- 1 CUP FLOUR—I PREFER WHITE LILY.
- 2–4 32-OUNCE BOXES OF CHICKEN STOCK—DOESN'T MATTER THE BRAND, THOUGH I DIG THE KITCHEN BASICS WHEN I CAN FIND IT. STORE BRAND IS FINE, TOO. YOU'LL FIND OUT IN A MINUTE WHY I SAY 2–4.
- HALF A CUP OF WORCESTERSHIRE—BRAND MATTERS HERE—GO WITH THE ORIGINAL, LEA & PERRINS. IF YOU AIN'T GOT ANY, GO BUY SOME!
- SOY SAUCE, BUT JUST A SPLASH.
- AT LEAST HALF A BOTTLE OF KETCHUP, AND IT'S GOTTA BE HEINZ. OTHERWISE IT'S JUST LIQUID TOMATOES.
- 4 PACKAGES OF HILLSHIRE KIELBASA. BRAND MATTERS HERE, TOO. GO WITH TWO POLSKA AND TWO BEEF.
- PAPER TOWELS FOR COVERING KIELBASA DURING THEIR TIME IN THE MICROWAVE.
- 2–3 BAY LEAVES.
- AN ENTIRE COOKED CHICKEN. IF TIME ALLOWS, GET A ROTISSERIE CHICKEN THE DAY OF. PUT IT ON THE COUNTER, NOT IN THE FRIDGE. YOU DON'T WANT IT COLD— THAT MAKES IT A BOOGER TO PULL APART. YOU'RE GOING TO ADD THIS TO THE SIMMERING GOODNESS ABOUT AN HOUR BEFORE SERVING.
- 4 POUNDS OF MEDIUM SHRIMP, BOILED AND PEELED. FINE TO DICE THEM, IF YOU LIKE.
- WHITE VINEGAR, TO ADD TO THE WATER IN WHICH YOU BOIL SAID PRAWNS.
- OLD BAY SEASONING, ALSO TO ADD TO THE WATER IN WHICH YOU BOIL SAID PRAWNS.
- YOU CAN ADD CRAB MEAT, BUT ONLY IF IT'S FRESH FROM THE CATCH. LUMP MEAT—NOT CLAW. PASTEURIZED WILL DO IN A PINCH, BUT YOUR TASTE BUDS WILL FEEL IT. I SAY NO TO CLAW BECAUSE CLAW MEAT FALLS APART TO THE POINT WHERE YOU WILL HAVE DIFFICULTY KNOWING IT'S IN THERE. CRAB IS DAMN EXPENSIVE. THAT'S A LOT OF MONEY TO SPEND TO GO UNNOTICED.

PREPARATION

With your mighty sharp knife, chop all the veggies: celery, onions, peppers, garlic, etc. Put 'em in a big Tupperware bowl or any bowl you can seal. Chopping can be done the night before, unless you want to hit the mimosas at brunch. If so, chop the day of.

By now, you should have that kickass pot or Dutch oven. The bigger the better. Le Creuset rocks the house—but you know that.

Let's start with the roux—no shortcuts here. Might take half an hour or so to get it where it needs to be, but it's time well spent. Like you got somewhere else to go.

Spray your big ol' pot with a cooking spray you trust. Add oil and flour. Turn on the stove to about 5 on the dial, medium heat. I don't care what you use to stir (though you know I love my metal whisk), but be prepared to stir religiously for a good half hour. When the roux turns the color of rust, you're ready to rock. Like Mötley Crüe—the early years, not the sell-out pop radio years.

Now add all the veggies and the pinches of thyme, the okra last, but by no means least. There is no gumbo without okra. Do NOT add any liquid yet (this includes drool from the anticipation of making the best gumbo ever).

Let the okra take over. You'll need to do a certain amount of stirring here, too.

You'll notice it getting all gooey at first. This is a *very* good sign. You'll be ready for the next step when you can bite into the celery and it is soft as a piece of Hubba Bubba! (A tip on the celery: Pour a little chicken stock on the chopped bits and microwave for about 6 minutes to hasten the softness and time spent over the stove.)

Speaking of—it's chicken stock time. I'm a brothy kinda dude. I want my gumbo to be closer to soup than stew. A little extra liquid in the serving bowl is what makes this caddy yard gumbo so indescribably good, and in my mind how gumbo was originally intended. You can also add some lemon pepper here, garlic salt, garlic pepper, splash of soy sauce, Worcestershire and/or beer—all of this is as you see fit, of course, so just add a touch at first.

You'll know if you need to add more as the cooking progresses. My guess is that you will—I almost always do.

Add the ketchup and stir a little more. Just squeeze it out the bottle—don't mess with measuring. Squeeze the Heinz out of it! I don't rock the splashes of hot sauce, but if you want to it won't hurt my feelings or the simmering goodness on your stove.

Kielbasa time.

Slice all four packages into about ¼ inch of thickness—like Tinkertoys. Here's another cool trick. Place the sliced kielbasa onto a microwavable plate as spread out as you can—with a paper towel underneath and a paper towel on top. Dinner plate button for a minute or so, depending on your micro. When done, take a fresh paper towel and sop up the kielbasa grease. Do this for the first three packages.

For the fourth, yes again on paper towels for the top and bottom but *don't* use a fresh one to sop this time. A little grease is good—keeps the blood sliding through your veins. When you're done, drop all the kielbasa in the pot and stir. Add the bay leaves. Stir a little more.

You're pretty much good to go now, but don't go just yet. You've got some admiring to do.

What else can I say to lead you to gumbo greatness?

If time allows (sometimes it does), make your gumbo the night before, pull it out of the fridge a few hours before serving, and warm it up low and slow. If you go low and slow, it really can't go too long.

Either way, add the shredded rotisserie chicken to your gumbo pot about an hour or so before serving, letting things coast until the dinner bell rings. Be sure and answer when it does.

The very last step is an optional one, but not for this southern boy.

As we did with the Low Country Boil, cook the shrimp separately, dashing Old Bay Seasoning and a splash of white vinegar into just a bit of water. With a good rolling boil, shrimp will cook in 3 minutes, usually less (yes, I know you know this). Don't add the shrimp to the gumbo warming on the stove lest they shrivel up like raisins. Serve 'em on the side and let folks add 'em to their bowl as desired.

So much better this way.

Speaking of bowls, if you can go the bread bowl route, then yowzah! is that ever good and a mighty nice presentation to boot. Panera Bread usually has them; Publix, too. They'll even carve 'em out for you, but I say carve 'em out yourself, like pumpkins at Halloween. Be a kid again.

Every chance you can.

MR. B. AND
SQUEEGEE McGEE

Winters in Augusta are curious things, like the backward-bending legs of an ostrich or pretty much all things duckbill platypus. One day it's 85° and sunny, and you're wearing shorts under your white caddy jumpsuit. The next it's 34° and raining—no amount of clothing will keep you warm, and every umbrella in the pro shop won't keep you dry. If you're caddying for Mr. B., which I was, you're in for one long-ass, miserable day, which I also was.

That doesn't mean you have to go hungry on such a cold and godforsaken day, and nothing warms the bones quite like a bowl of caddy house chili, made in our house and now served in yours. But that was three recipes ago, and the only thing in my belly right now is the desire to leave you with one last story from a time in my life that was as magical as it was surreal.

It was also one hell of a lot of fun.

Caddy's Log, Stardate February 24, 1993, Augusta National Golf Club.

Mr. B. and me, and we're the last ones standing.

When we teed off that morning, we were eight men strong. When we made the turn, we were two, one of us less strong than the other. The rest of our group had thrown in their frozen, wet towels after just seven holes. Even Melvin, the angry-at-the-world halfway house cart guy had called it quits before making fun of our soaking wet selves.

Bunch'a candy asses.

Easy for me to say, with my own candy-ass melting like MacArthur's Park in the dark, with all the sweet green icing flowing down. Someone left the cake out in the rain, and the poor ol' caddy, too.

That poor ol' caddy was me.

As Mr. B. and I sloshed our way to the 10th tee like Washington crossing the Delaware with holes in the raft, I thought if I were any wetter I'd be the ocean, any colder and I'd be Maria from the seventh grade, who wouldn't give you the time of day even if it was on her side.

With the rain coming down like God crying at *Old Yeller*, Mr. B. trades me his umbrella for his driver, a beautiful old, wooden Toney Penna that's seen a lot of fairways. With nine pars on the scorecard—yes, that crazy old lovable coot just shot even par in the freezing rain at Augusta—Mr. B. is happy as a Jack-in-the-Box with the lid open. He's also pointing down the 10th fairway, at the green in the distance. *Way* in the distance.

I squint to try and decipher the objects, but with rain-watered eyes they look like yellow slabs of butter.

Yellow slabs of butter wearing head to toe rain slickers and pushing squeegees! My God in Heaven. The entire squee-gee grounds crew (yes, Augusta has one), is squeegeeing the greens for one man. I would pinch myself to make sure I'm not dreaming, but I'm so cold I'd never feel it.

I look at my feet, soaked as pool towels,

then up and see nothing but green. Just like that, the squeegee boys are gone.

Except, they're not.

After Mr. B. taps in for one hell of a rain-soaked par, we swap putter for driver and umbrella, and I shortcut my way around the back of 10 green and slog through a cloister of azaleas, waiting for Mr. B. to stripe his drive. Of course, he's going to stripe it. He hasn't missed a fairway all morning!

I turn left to face the music. I catch Mr. B.'s ball flight and follow as it splashes onto the middle of the fairway and rooster tails to a stop, as do I. Dead in my tracks.

If I were anywhere else, I wouldn't believe my eyes. But I'm not. I'm at Augusta National, the original Magic Kingdom. Sorry, Walt. You're a day late and a Mickey Mouse short.

As synchronized as swimmers, the yellow-cladded squeegee team make short work of the 11th green. They take a little longer on the 12th, the lowest point on the golf course. Still, when we reach the green it's as if it never rained at all.

We follow the squeegee boys around shot for shot, step for step, squeegee for squeegee, until we walk off 18 green with an even par 36 to bookend our 36 on the front.

Mr. B. is thrilled, and he thanks his very own squeegee crew with a grin like a banana. As the squeegee boys get back in their E-Z-GOs, they smile and wave like the Madagascar penguins.

"Hell of a round, there, Mr. B.," says the

squeegee lead dog, his scenery finally changing. "Honored to be a part of that one."

Me, too, I say to myself, and in a way that's hard to explain, I am. *Squeegeeing greens 10–18, just for one man and his water-logged caddy.*

Was it a little over the top? Yeah, a little.

The privileges of membership? Sure. But was it pretty damn cool? Yeah, it was pretty damn cool.

Every last bit of it.

AFTERWORD:
CADDY'S DELIGHT SOUP

BY THE REV. DR. JOE BOWDEN,
PERSONAL PHYSICIAN TO THE CADDIES OF
AUGUSTA NATIONAL GOLF CLUB FOR OVER 40 YEARS

My son Tripper, writer and former Augusta National caddy, is generous. Some would say he is generous to a fault—I agree with that. Tripp is especially generous in giving away things that don't belong to him.

In an odd way, that generosity led to the creation of the short-lived culinary legend known as Caddy's Delight Soup.

This heartwarming story begins in the late 1980s.

Having run out of courses to take, Tripp graduated with a degree in English and minors in philosophy and psychology from Augusta College (now Augusta University). Tripp's first post-graduation job was caddying at Augusta National Golf Club, and during this time Tripp still lived at home.

But we'll get back to Tripp—now, a little bit about me.

As Tripp was drifting nicely into caddy life, I was drifting heels-dug-in into my forties—the dreaded time of a midlife crisis. My youth was in the memories of medical school, surgical residency, and military service. I knew I could not reclaim my youth, but maybe, just maybe, I could hold on to what was left. However, the mirror had condemned me with a most dreaded disease—*the chest of drawers malady.*

My chest had fallen into my drawers.

You know the rest of the story, as it is all too familiar with us midlife crisis folk—I started running and working out in a desperate attempt to turn back the hands of time. In truth, I was never all that committed to the "working out" part of the equation. I had always subscribed to the Mark Twain School of Exercise, and it fit me like a good pair of walking shoes.

"Whenever I get the urge to exercise, I lie down until the feeling passes away."

As a physician, I knew well the complex formula for losing weight. Thousands of people have gotten rich selling weight-loss books. You may have bought one. Don't feel guilty.

Well, I'm going to give you the answer: "Eat less! Exercise more!" No need to thank me, just buy this book and recommend it to your friends.

But what, exactly, should one eat?

The answer to that 64-dollar question came from my growing-up days on the farm in the '40s. My grandparents were sharecroppers, which, for any millennial reading this, means you worked the land, but you didn't own it. My family raised or grew just about everything that appeared on the dinner table, and we were blessed to have it.

Everyone had responsibilities to see there was something on the table for every meal, and my job was threefold: see to the chickens, keep any and all dogs out of the house, and plant—with adult supervision—the cabbage patch. Once planted, I was the lord of the cabbage patch, which in farm speak means watering, weeding, and fertilizing.

Take that, your lordship!

Now, cabbages love organic material, better known as manure. And I loved my cabbage patch—it thrived because of me! It was some years later that I learned just how hardy is the cabbage. Beyond planting the seeds, I actually had very little influence on its eventual success.

With that, step 1 to reclaiming my youth was complete. *Cabbage* was the answer to my midlife crisis. Eat a lot of cabbage, lead a sedentary life, lose weight. Perfect!

Except, it's not.

Eating a lot of *just cabbage* is not the winning formula for a weight-loss program designed to last more than a few days. The solitary cabbage, like each of us, needs companions. Herein lies the endless journey without a permanent destination that is cabbage soup.

Fast forward a few ticks of the clock. (Yes, I stole that line from my son.)

In the fall of '89, my cabbage soup and the Augusta National caddies converged. I had experimented with a variety of tasty things to add to my cabbage cauldron—some tastier than others. It was a Tuesday night when I finished a pot of cabbage soup that I thought just might be my *opus magnus*. The "secret" was diced hot dogs and chopped bacon.

I couldn't wait to come home from work the next day to have a lunch fit for a king, a meal of which surely, I was worthy.

When I arrived home the following day,

there were several cars in the driveway I did not recognize. As I walked into the house I saw gathered around the kitchen table two foursomes of caddies, still in their white jumpsuits and green hats. In the center of the table was my large pot of cabbage soup. It was nearly empty.

Tripp, in his aforementioned endless generosity, had invited his new caddy friends over to "his house" for a lunch of the good doctor's great soup. I couldn't get mad at all the caddies whom I had known as patients and friends for many years, and I certainly couldn't fault Tripp's generosity, so I pulled up a chair and enjoyed the last of my soup, which was mostly pot liquor by then.

It was, however, one of the greatest meals of my life.

We told stories, laughed, and just enjoyed being together. At the end of this memorable breaking of bread, a defining statement was made by one of Augusta's longtime caddies named Pee Wee, who had been caddying at Augusta for as long as he—and I—could remember.

Pee Wee sat back in his chair, wiped his satisfied chin with a paper towel, and said, "Doc, that soup was *delightful!*"

And, with that, my soup now had a name—*Caddy's Delight*!

From that moment forward and until Tripp moved on to other things, I always kept a big ol' pot of various renditions of *Caddy's Delight Soup* in the back fridge. Tripp, still living at home with no sense of urgency to live anywhere else, always knew when the pot was full. As strange as it may sound, I always smiled when I came home at the end of the day and the soup pot was empty.

Please don't think I made all this soup for the caddies, though it gladdened my heart to know they would have at least one good meal beyond breakfast. I always put some soup aside for myself, in a Tupperware container I kept in the front refrigerator, labeled: *Rutabagas—all you can eat.*

My share of the soup was safe.

I welcome you to create your own recipe for Caddy's Delight Soup. As my son Tripper likes to say: Now, go, and make it your own! One ingredient you absolutely need is a cabbage. The other is imagination.

When you have completed your masterpiece, invite some friends or caddies over. I promise you the time together will be, in a word that means so much more than just its definition, delightful. But don't waste precious time looking it up.

This one is meant to be lived.

"The whole point of taking pictures is so that you don't have to explain things with words."
—Elliott Erwitt

PHOTO CREDITS

Page x Fletch Bowden
Page xii-xiii iStock
Page xviii Associated Press
Page 10 iStock
Page 22 iStock
Page 42 iStock
Page 44 Rev. Dr. Joe Bowden
Page 68 iStock
Page 94 iStock
Page 124 Tripp Bowden
Page 142 Associated Press
Page 196 iStock
Page 206 Marion Cotton

*Remaining photographs by Judah Gutierrez

ACKNOWLEDGMENTS

If brevity is the soul of wit, then where does that leave me?
—Tripp Bowden

Life is too short to stuff a mushroom.
—Shirley Conran, author of *Superwoman*

If you only had five minutes to thank the people in your life that matter the most, could you do it? If so, who would they be?

Hell of a question.

Thank God I don't have to answer it here. Not now, anyway, and certainly not in such an unrealistic time frame. Speaking of—you got a minute?

There are indeed some folks I must thank—because without them this book would be just another idea (world is full of those, you know?), and not one whose time has come.

A dear friend once said to me: "Tripper, if you can't act on the moment, then get off the stage."

Exit stage left, my ass. But, man, these spotlights are bright. Imagine if they were the light shining down from everyone who believes in you?

Oh, wait.

They are.

To Fletch, the love of my life, for being the brightest light of them all. For second chances and your boundless, unconditional love. Your belief in me is what leads me to believe. *None* of this happens without you.

To Arrie B and Holly Mac—every day you teach me there is still so much I have to learn, then you show me through morning hugs and goodnight kisses that maybe, *just* maybe, ol' Squaddy/Daddy is doing something right after all.

To Bobby and Wendy, for opening your home and lending an ear—sorry, you can't have it back—when I was a lost voice in the wilderness. You know the tree that falls in the forest, when no one's around to hear it? It actually *does* make a sound. Because of you, I was around to hear it.

To Shakes, for your couch and uncommon friendship. There really is no place like home—thanks for sharing yours with me.

To Big E, for your endless sea of "wit me or agin mes." Looks like I'm wit ye for the long haul, you jackass.

To Gaff, for always being Gaff. I think Gaff is Latin for Rock of Gibraltar. In fact, I'm sure of it.

To Dr. Walter Evans, my writing mentor. I know to dub you thusly makes you cringe and laugh—best laugh ever, by the way. Thank you, Dr. Evans, for teaching me the most important of all writing lessons: there is no such thing as writing, only rewriting. Thanks to your teachings, I fear no blank page, though I will always fear your red felt pen.

Oh, I felt it, all right. A marked-up, ink-slashed copy of *How I Spent My Summer* read aloud in front of a class of strangers will change a man (to borrow a classic line from *Rango*).

To Eminem—as go your lyrics, so do I. I'm not afraid. Not anymore. To Stephen King, thanks to you I'm not out there "washing the car"; to Mitch Albom, thank you for teaching me the gravitational heartstring pull of a properly placed line break; and to the inimitable Lawrence Sanders, for teaching me the infinite effectiveness of fearless description. *Penis in worm-eaten walnut* is perhaps the greatest line of all time.

One more (isn't there always one more?), and that is to Pat Conroy, for not being afraid to tell your life story while still very much alive. There is no death when you can pull that off, certainly not one with sting. There have been none better at that than you.

To Alice Sebold (told you there's always one more), who earth-bounds the ethereal like no other writer I know. *The Lovely Bones* is the most beautiful book I've ever read.

To my sister Jote, for teaching me laughter really is the best medicine, no matter how sick the joke (keep it clean, kids)—or the patient. To Tone, for following suit. Thanks, my good man.

To my dear cousin Kathy, for keeping the bloodlines flowing, the belief in earth angels heavenly, and for watering the family tree.

To Mum and Peter, for your unconditional love and unwavering belief in me yesterday, today, and always. A baby boy can carry a mighty heavy load with Kubotas like you on his side.

To Pop, for genetically (or is that phonetically?) bequeathing in me your timeless sense of humor, quick wit, and generous soul. And to Mimi, who said without words that I could do better (you were right), so I did. I should be sorry for having the word "ass" in a cookbook, but the funny thing is I'm not.

That one's for you, Ma Otter.

To Hot Shot and Sweet Pete, for short leg lambs and au revoir potatoes. Tereshinski!

To Jarbs, for saying I'm his inspiration—when in fact it's the other way around. There's a lot to be said for the other way around, though, especially if that's the way you're going.

To Judah, for your incredible gift with the lens—yours *and* the camera's. Brother, you got mad skills. To the always smiling Azia, for opening your eclectic home on sleepy Sundays—best natural light through kitchen windows ever!—and to Elena, the bad-ass stylist, whose style is all her own.

This doesn't work without y'all.

To my editor, Julie, who knows my writing like da Vinci knows the code. Julie, you know just when to release the Kraken and when to keep him in the castle. Few editors have that gift.

To the good folks at Skyhorse: Bill W. for opening another door, Tony for always keeping it cracked (just in case), the design team for putting up with my seemingly (ha!) endless tweaks, and to Sarah, for navigating the shipping lanes (your emails always smile).

To Freddie, for sharing your infinite wisdom with me and all those blessed to have known you. Thanks, Freddie. For everything.

To Chef James Clark, for making complicated cooking look easy, because, well, maybe it is.

We should *all* thank you for that.

To my caddy brothers at Augusta National Golf Club, I thank you for welcoming me as one of your own, for taking me under your collective wing, for giving me a place to call home and a purpose in life when I so desperately needed one. I'll never forget that—nor, will I ever forget you. And to Doc Durst, a friend to all caddies great and small.

And to those out there trying to get right with the bottle, it's OK if your life turns upside down in the process. Sometimes you gotta go forward to get back to square one.

My last thank-you is to God. It's true, you know. With God, all things are possible. You're holding the proof in your hands. Catch those dreams, y'all.

I hear kitchen string makes a pretty good lasso.